All New
Diabetic Choices

Publications International Ltd.

Favorite Brand Name Recipes at www.fbnr.com

Copyright © 2002 Publications International, Ltd.
Recipes and text copyright © 2002 KF Holdings, Inc.
All rights reserved. This publication may not be reproduced or quoted in whole or in part by any means whatsoever without written permission from:

Louis Weber, CEO
Publications International, Ltd.
7373 North Cicero Avenue
Lincolnwood, IL 60712

Permission is never granted for commercial purposes.

ANGEL FLAKE, BAKER'S, BREAKSTONE'S, CALUMET, CATALINA, COOL WHIP, COOL WHIP LITE, COUNTRY TIME, CRYSTAL LIGHT, CRYSTAL LIGHT TROPICAL PASSIONS, FREE, GENERAL FOODS INTERNATIONAL COFFEES, GERMAN'S, GOOD SEASONS, JELL-O, KNUDSEN, KOOL-AID, KRAFT, LIGHT DONE RIGHT, MAXWELL HOUSE, MINUTE, OSCAR MAYER, PHILADELPHIA, POST, POST SELECTS, POST SPOON SIZE, TANG and VELVEETA LIGHT are registered trademarks of KF Holdings, Inc., Northfield, IL 60093.

TACO BELL® and HOME ORIGINALS® are registered trademarks owned and licensed by Taco Bell Corp.

Breyers® is a registered trademark if Unilever, N.V., used under license.

BOCA™ is trademark of BOCA Foods Company.

Recipe Development: Kraft Kitchens
Recipe Nutrition: Kraft Foods, Registered Dietitians
Project Coordination: Kraft Diabetic Partnership

Photography: Stephen Hamilton Photographics, Inc.
Photographers: Stephen Hamilton, Tate Hunt
Photographers' Assistant: Tom Guida   **Prop Stylist:** Paula Walters
Food Stylists: Walter Moeller, Judy Vance   **Assistant Food Stylist:** Lisa Knych

Pictured on the front cover: Chicken Brown Rice Primavera *(page 24)*.

ISBN-13: 978-0-7853-6312-5
ISBN-10: 0-7853-6312-2

Manufactured in China.

8 7 6 5 4 3 2 1

Nutritional Analysis: Nutritional information is given for the recipes in this publication. Each analysis is based on the food items in the ingredient list, except ingredients labeled as "optional" or "as desired." When more than one ingredient choice is listed, the first ingredient is used for analysis. Nutrition claims are based on criteria set forth in government regulations for nutrition labeling of foods. Exchange calculations are based on Exchange Lists for Meal Planning, © 1995, the American Diabetes Association, Inc., and the American Dietetic Association.

Preparation/Cooking Times: Preparation times are based on the approximate amount of time required to assemble the recipe before cooking, baking, chilling or serving. These times include preparation steps such as measuring, chopping and mixing. The fact that some preparations and cooking can be done simultaneously is taken into account. Preparation of optional ingredients and serving suggestions is not included.

CONTENTS

INTRODUCTION	6
BREAKFAST & BRUNCH	8
MAIN DISHES	18
SALADS & SIDE DISHES	32
DESSERTS	46
BEVERAGES	68
SNACKS & DIPS	80
INDEX	93

**Visit us on the web at
www.kraftdiabeticchoices.com**

INTRODUCTION

A Note of Thanks from Kraft Diabetic Choices

Thank you for your enthusiastic response to our first *Kraft Diabetic Choices* cookbook! I think all of us agree that eating right and being active are important to feeling good today and in the future. But, like you, I sometimes find that my health goals get set aside as I try to keep up with the many demands of everyday living. So we've created a whole new lineup of easy and delicious recipes in this second edition of the *Kraft Diabetic Choices* cookbook.

Why not try the Chicken Brown Rice Primavera tonight (page 24; cover photo)—a fast, flavorful dish with grains, meat and veggies all in one. In the mood for a sweet treat? It's hard to pick with so many mouth-watering choices, but we've created every one to help you eat right! Try the Lemon Soufflé Cheesecake (page 48)—no one will guess it's low fat. Or, try easy-to-make Peanut Butter and Jam Parfaits (page 64) and discover a dessert everyone will love.

Enjoy this edition of the *Kraft Diabetic Choices* cookbook, and please write me at carol@kraftfoods.com to share your ideas.

Here's to your health,

Carol

Carol Altomare, RD
Registered Dietitian,
Kraft Kitchens

INTRODUCTION

Recipe Nutrition Know-How

Recipes in this book were developed according to nutrition recommendations set forth by the American Diabetes Association. Each recipe lists nutrition information per serving for calories, fat, carbohydrate and protein. Many recipes contain good-for-you nutrients, like fiber, vitamin A, vitamin C, calcium and iron. Exchange values are also given so you can see how a recipe can fit into your eating plan.

Some recipes are highlighted with special symbols, indicating they are low in fat or calories or good sources of fiber or calcium.

 **Low Calorie:** contains 40 calories or less per reference amount*

 **Low Fat:** contains 3 grams or less of fat per reference amount

 **Contains Fiber:** contains 10% or more of the daily value for fiber per reference amount

 **Good Source of Calcium:** contains 10% or more of the daily value for calcium per reference amount

 **Low Sodium:** contains 140 grams or less of sodium per reference amount

Reference amount is specified by the government for food categories and is the basis for serving size.

For main dishes and meals 120 calories or less per reference amount.

Check Us Out!

Visit us at www.kraftdiabeticchoices.com to get more great recipes and nutrition information. You are just a click away from meal-planning tools, seasonal features, recipe contests and links to other web sites about diabetes. Let us show you how easy it is to rely on Kraft for food products that turn your meal plan into delicious results your whole family will enjoy.

7

Breakfast & Brunch

Breakfast Quesadilla

Prep: 5 minutes   Cook: 4 minutes

1 frozen BOCA Breakfast Patty *or* 2 frozen BOCA Breakfast Links
1 TACO BELL® HOME ORIGINALS® Flour Tortilla
1 tablespoon PHILADELPHIA Light Cream Cheese Spread
TACO BELL® HOME ORIGINALS® Thick 'N Chunky Salsa (optional)

HEAT breakfast patty or links as directed on package.

SPREAD flour tortilla with cream cheese. Top with chopped patty or links; fold tortilla in half.

HEAT tortilla in nonstick or lightly oiled skillet on medium heat about 2 minutes on each side. Serve with salsa, if desired.

Makes 1 serving

Nutrition Information Per Serving: 220 calories, 9g total fat, 2.5g saturated fat, 10mg cholesterol, 560mg sodium, 22g carbohydrate, 4g dietary fiber, 3g sugars, 12g protein

10% daily value calcium, 10% daily value iron

Exchange: 1½ Starch, 1 Lean Meat, 1 Fat

BREAKFAST & BRUNCH

Lemony Wheatful Fruit Bread

Prep: 10 minutes   Bake: 50 minutes

½ cup (1 stick) margarine, melted
½ cup fat free milk
2 eggs
   Finely grated peel from 1 lemon
2 tablespoons lemon juice
1 cup sugar
2 cups flour
1½ cups POST SPOON SIZE Shredded Wheat Cereal, finely crushed
1 teaspoon baking soda
¼ teaspoon ground cinnamon
1 cup dried fruit mix (such as prune, apricot, pear), chopped

HEAT oven to 350°F. Spray 9×5-inch loaf pan with no stick cooking spray.

MIX margarine, milk, eggs, lemon peel, juice and sugar in large bowl until well blended. Stir in flour, crushed cereal, baking soda and cinnamon until blended. Stir in fruit. Pour into prepared pan.

BAKE 50 minutes or until bread is golden brown and toothpick inserted in center comes out clean. Cool 10 minutes; remove from pan. Cool completely on wire rack. Store wrapped in plastic wrap.

Makes 1 loaf or 12 (¾-inch) slices

Nutrition Information Per Serving (¾-inch slice): 280 calories, 9g total fat, 1.5g saturated fat, 35mg cholesterol, 200mg sodium, 47g carbohydrate, 2g dietary fiber, 24g sugars, 5g protein

15% daily value vitamin A, 10% daily value iron

Exchange: 1½ Starch, 1½ Fruit, 1½ Fat

BREAKFAST & BRUNCH

Waffle Stack

Prep: 5 minutes

  2 toasted waffles
½ cup BREAKSTONE'S *or* KNUDSEN 2% Cottage Cheese
10 strawberry slices
  2 kiwi slices
¼ cup mixed raspberries and blueberries

SPREAD 1 waffle with cottage cheese; top with second waffle spread with cottage cheese. Top with fruit.

Makes 1 serving

Nutrition Information Per Serving: 300 calories, 8g total fat, 2.5g saturated fat, 30mg cholesterol, 920mg sodium, 41g carbohydrate, 5g dietary fiber, 21g sugars, 17g protein

20% daily value vitamin A, 80% daily value vitamin C, 25% daily value calcium

Exchange: 2 Starch, ½ Fruit, 2 Lean Meat

BREAKFAST & BRUNCH

Applesauce Muffins

Prep: 10 minutes   Bake: 20 minutes

1¼ cups flour
1 tablespoon CALUMET Baking Powder
¼ teaspoon salt
2 cups POST Fruit & Fiber Cereal
1 cup fat free milk
1 egg
½ cup applesauce
⅓ cup firmly packed brown sugar
2 tablespoons margarine, melted

HEAT oven to 400°F. Spray muffin pan with no stick cooking spray.

MIX flour, baking powder and salt in large bowl. Mix cereal and milk in small bowl; let stand 3 minutes.

BEAT egg in another small bowl; stir in applesauce, sugar and margarine. Stir into cereal mixture. Add to flour mixture; stir just until moistened. (Batter will be lumpy.) Spoon batter into prepared muffin pan, filling each cup ⅔ full.

BAKE 20 minutes or until golden brown. Serve warm.

Makes 12 muffins

Storage Know-How: Store completely cooled muffins in airtight container up to 2 days.

Nutrition Information Per Muffin: 150 calories, 3g total fat, 0.5g saturated fat, 20mg cholesterol, 260mg sodium, 26g carbohydrate, 1g dietary fiber, 11g sugars, 3g protein

10% daily value calcium, 10% daily value iron

Exchange: 1½ Starch, ½ Fat

BREAKFAST & BRUNCH

Double Apple Bran Cereal Muffins

Prep: 10 minutes   Bake: 20 minutes

1¼ cups flour
1 tablespoon CALUMET Baking Powder
¼ teaspoon ground cinnamon
¼ teaspoon salt
2 cups POST Bran Flakes Cereal
1 cup fat free milk
1 egg
1 small apple, peeled, cored and finely chopped
½ cup applesauce
⅓ cup firmly packed brown sugar
2 tablespoons margarine, melted

HEAT oven to 400°F. Spray muffin pan with no stick cooking spray.

MIX flour, baking powder, cinnamon and salt in large bowl. Mix cereal and milk in another bowl; let stand 3 minutes.

BEAT egg in small bowl; stir in chopped apple, applesauce, sugar and margarine. Stir into cereal mixture. Add to flour mixture; stir just until moistened. (Batter will be lumpy.) Spoon batter into prepared muffin pan, filling each cup ⅔ full. Bake 20 minutes or until golden brown. Serve warm.

Makes 12 muffins

Nutrition Information Per Muffin: 140 calories, 2.5g total fat, 0.5g saturated fat, 20mg cholesterol, 260mg sodium, 26g carbohydrate, 2g dietary fiber, 11g sugars, 3g protein

10% daily value calcium, 15% daily value iron

Exchange: 1½ Starch, ½ Fat

Breakfast & Brunch

Low Fat Orange-Raisin Bran Bread

Prep: 10 minutes   Bake: 60 minutes

1½ cups flour
1 cup sugar
1 tablespoon CALUMET Baking Powder
¼ teaspoon salt
1 egg
¾ cup fat free milk
½ cup orange juice
2 tablespoons oil
2 tablespoons grated orange peel
2 cups POST Bran Flakes
¾ cup raisins

HEAT oven to 350°F. Spray 9×5-inch loaf pan with no stick cooking spray.

MIX flour, sugar, baking powder and salt in large bowl.

BEAT egg in small bowl; stir in milk, orange juice, oil and orange peel. Add to flour mixture; stir just until moistened. (Batter will be lumpy.) Stir in cereal and raisins. Pour into prepared loaf pan.

BAKE 55 to 60 minutes or until toothpick inserted in center comes out clean. Cool 10 minutes; remove from pan. Cool completely on wire rack.

Makes 1 loaf or 18 (½-inch) slices

Nutrition Information Per Serving (½-inch slice): 140 calories, 2g total fat, 0g saturated fat, 10mg cholesterol, 135mg sodium, 29g carbohydrate, 1g dietary fiber, 17g sugars, 2g protein

10% daily value iron

Exchange: 2 Starch

BREAKFAST & BRUNCH

Breakfast Burrito

Prep: 10 minutes   Cook: 10 minutes

   1 cup fat free cholesterol free refrigerated egg product
  ¼ cup fat free milk
   2 green onions, sliced
   3 BOCA Frozen Breakfast Patties, coarsely chopped *or* broken apart
  ½ cup KRAFT 2% Milk Shredded Colby & Monterey Jack Cheese
   4 TACO BELL® HOME ORIGINALS® Flour Tortillas, heated
     TACO BELL® HOME ORIGINALS® Salsa (optional)

BEAT egg product and milk in medium bowl. Add onions and patty pieces.

COOK egg mixture in nonstick or lightly oiled medium skillet on medium heat until set. Top with cheese; cover until melted.

SPOON a scant ½ cup egg mixture onto each warm tortilla. Fold in ends and roll-up burrito style. Serve immediately. Serve with salsa, if desired.

Makes 4 servings

Nutrition Information Per Serving: 270 calories, 10g total fat, 3g saturated fat, 10mg cholesterol, 650mg sodium, 22g carbohydrate, 3g dietary fiber, 3g sugars, 20g protein

30% daily value vitamin A, 30% daily value calcium, 20% daily value iron

Exchange: 1½ Starch, 2 Lean Meat, 1 Fat

Main Dishes

Nugget Parmigiana Sub
Prep: 5 minutes

    4 frozen BOCA Chik'n Nuggets
    1 small (2 ounce) submarine roll, split
  ¼ cup spaghetti sauce, heated
    1 tablespoon KRAFT 2% Milk Shredded Reduced Fat Mozzarella Cheese
    1 tablespoon KRAFT Reduced Fat Parmesan Style Grated Topping

HEAT nuggets as directed on package.

PLACE nuggets in sub roll. Top with warm spaghetti sauce.

SPRINKLE with mozzarella and Parmesan topping.

Makes 1 sandwich

Nutrition Information Per Serving: 500 calories, 15g total fat, 3.5g saturated fat, 15mg cholesterol, 1480mg sodium, 63g carbohydrate, 6g dietary fiber, 9g sugars, 27g protein

20% daily value vitamin A, 10% daily value vitamin C, 35% daily value calcium, 20% daily value iron

Exchange: 4 Starch, 2 Lean Meat, 2 Fat

MAIN DISHES

Spinach Lasagna

Prep: 25 minutes   **Bake:** 45 minutes plus standing

1 container (16 ounces) BREAKSTONE'S or KNUDSEN 2% Cottage Cheese
1 package (10 ounces) frozen chopped spinach, thawed, well drained
2 cups KRAFT Shredded Low-Moisture Part Skim Mozzarella Cheese, divided
½ cup KRAFT Reduced Fat Parmesan Style Grated Topping, divided
1 egg, beaten
1 jar (28 ounces) spaghetti sauce, divided
6 lasagna noodles, cooked, drained

HEAT oven to 350°F.

MIX cottage cheese, spinach, 1 cup of the mozzarella cheese, ¼ cup of the grated topping and egg.

LAYER 1 cup of the spaghetti sauce, ½ of the lasagna noodles and ½ of the cottage cheese mixture in 13×9-inch baking dish. Repeat layers, ending with sauce. Sprinkle with remaining 1 cup mozzarella cheese and ¼ cup of the Parmesan topping.

BAKE 45 minutes. Let stand 10 minutes before serving.

Makes 10 servings

Nutrition Information Per Serving: 280 calories, 11g total fat, 4.5g saturated fat, 45mg cholesterol, 890mg sodium, 30g carbohydrate, 4g dietary fiber, 10g sugars, 16g protein

70% daily value vitamin A, 25% daily value vitamin C, 30% daily value calcium, 10% daily value iron

Exchange: 2 Starch, 1 Very Lean Meat, 2 Fat

MAIN DISHES

VELVEETA LIGHT® Easy Pasta Primavera

Prep: 15 minutes   Cook: 20 minutes

3 cups (8 ounces) rotini, uncooked
2 cups water
1 package (16 ounces) frozen vegetable blend
½ pound (8 ounces) VELVEETA LIGHT Pasteurized Prepared Cheese Product, cut up
¼ teaspoon garlic powder
¼ teaspoon pepper

BRING pasta and water to boil in saucepan; simmer 10 minutes or until pasta is tender.

ADD vegetables, prepared cheese product and seasonings. Stir until prepared cheese product is melted and mixture is thoroughly heated.

Makes 6 (1-cup) servings

Nutrition Information Per Serving: 340 calories, 7g total fat, 4g saturated fat, 25mg cholesterol, 890mg sodium, 50g carbohydrate, 3g dietary fiber, 9g sugars, 19g protein

25% daily value vitamin A, 45% daily value vitamin C, 35% daily value calcium, 10% daily value iron

Exchange: 3 Starch, 1 Vegetable, 1 Lean Meat, ½ Fat

Main Dishes

Down Home Macaroni & Cheese

Prep: 10 minutes   Bake: 20 minutes

   2 tablespoons margarine, divided
   ¼ cup flour
   ¼ teaspoon salt
   2 cups fat free milk
   ¼ pound (4 ounces) VELVEETA LIGHT Pasteurized Prepared Cheese Product, cut up
   1 package (8 ounces) KRAFT FREE Shredded Non Fat Cheddar Cheese, divided
   2 cups (8 ounces) elbow macaroni, cooked, drained
   2 tablespoons seasoned dry bread crumbs

HEAT oven to 350°F.

MELT 1 tablespoon margarine in saucepan on low heat. Blend in flour and salt; cook and stir 1 minute. Gradually add milk; cook, stirring constantly, until thickened. Add prepared cheese product and 1½ cups of the shredded cheese; stir until melted. Stir in macaroni.

POUR into 1½-quart casserole. Melt remaining 1 tablespoon margarine; toss with bread crumbs. Sprinkle casserole with remaining shredded cheese and bread crumb mixture.

BAKE 20 minutes or until thoroughly heated.

Makes 6 (1-cup) servings

Nutrition Information Per Serving: 320 calories, 7g total fat, 2.5g saturated fat, 15mg cholesterol, 880mg sodium, 40g carbohydrate, 2g dietary fiber, 7g sugars, 24g protein

25% daily value vitamin A, 60% daily value calcium,

Exchange: 2½ Starch, 2 Lean Meat

Main Dishes

Chicken Brown Rice Primavera

Prep: 15 minutes   Cook: 20 minutes

 1 tablespoon oil
 ¾ pound boneless skinless chicken breasts, cut into strips
 2 cloves garlic, minced
1½ cups chicken broth
 1 cup broccoli flowerets
 ½ red pepper, cut into strips
 ½ cup diagonally sliced carrot
 ½ cup sliced yellow squash
 ¼ teaspoon black pepper
1½ cups MINUTE Instant Brown Rice, uncooked
 ¼ cup (1 ounce) KRAFT 100% Grated Parmesan Cheese

HEAT oil in large skillet on medium-high heat. Add chicken and garlic; cook and stir until chicken is lightly browned.

ADD broth, broccoli, red pepper, carrot, squash and black pepper. Bring to boil.

STIR in rice. Return to boil. Reduce heat to low; cover and simmer 5 minutes. Remove from heat. Let stand 5 minutes. Stir in cheese.

Makes 4 servings

Nutrition Information Per Serving: 330 calories, 9g total fat, 3g saturated fat, 55mg cholesterol, 790mg sodium, 31g carbohydrate, 3g dietary fiber, 2g sugars, 31g protein

100% daily value vitamin A, 70% daily value vitamin C, 15% daily value calcium, 10% daily value iron

Exchange: 2 Starch, 1 Vegetable, 3 Very Lean Meat, 1 Fat

Main Dishes

BOCA® Chili

Prep: 10 minutes   Cook: 45 minutes

2 bell peppers (red, yellow *or* green), diced into ½-inch pieces
1 medium onion, chopped (about ½ cup)
2 cloves garlic, minced
2 teaspoons oil
1 box (12 ounces) frozen BOCA Crumbles
1 can (15 ounces) black beans, drained
1 can (15 ounces) chili beans in sauce
1 can (15 ounces) tomato sauce
1 can (14½ ounces) diced tomatoes
1 can (4 ounces) chopped green chilies, drained
1 tablespoon chili powder
½ teaspoon ground cumin

COOK and stir peppers, onion and garlic with oil in large saucepan on medium-high heat 2 minutes. Stir in crumbles; heat 2 to 3 minutes. Add remaining ingredients. Bring to boil; reduce heat.

SIMMER 30 minutes, stirring occasionally. Serve with your favorite chili toppings, if desired.

Makes 8 (1-cup) servings

Nutrition Information Per Serving: 210 calories, 2.5g total fat, 0g saturated fat, 0mg cholesterol, 960mg sodium, 33g carbohydrate, 12g dietary fiber, 7g sugars, 17g protein

60% daily value vitamin A, 80% daily value vitamin C, 10% daily value calcium, 20% daily value iron

Exchange: 2 Starch, 2 Vegetable, 1 Very Lean Meat

Main Dishes

20 Minute Garlic Rosemary Chicken & Brown Rice Dinner

Prep/Cook Time: 20 minutes

1 tablespoon oil
4 small boneless skinless chicken breast halves (about 1 pound)
¾ teaspoon garlic powder, divided
¾ teaspoon dried rosemary leaves, crushed, divided
1 can (10½ ounces) ⅓ less sodium chicken broth (1⅓ cups)
⅓ cup water
2 cups MINUTE Brown Rice, uncooked

HEAT oil in large nonstick skillet on medium-high heat. Add chicken; sprinkle with ¼ teaspoon each of the garlic powder and rosemary. Cover. Cook 4 minutes on each side or until cooked through. Remove chicken from skillet.

ADD broth and water to skillet; stir. Bring to boil.

STIR in rice and remaining ½ teaspoon each garlic powder and rosemary. Top with chicken; cover. Cook on low heat 5 minutes. Remove from heat. Let stand 5 minutes.

Makes 4 servings

Nutrition Information Per Serving: 340 calories, 7g total fat, 1g saturated fat, 70mg cholesterol, 290mg sodium, 36g carbohydrate, 2g dietary fiber, 0g sugars, 31g protein

Exchange: 2½ Starch, 3 Very Lean Meat, ½ Fat

MAIN DISHES

BOCA® Pasta Bake

Prep: 15 minutes   **Bake:** 30 minutes

1 box (12 ounces) frozen BOCA Crumbles
8 ounces mostaccioli, cooked and drained
1 jar (28 to 30 ounces) spaghetti sauce
¾ cup KRAFT Reduced Fat Parmesan Style Grated Topping, divided
1 package (8 ounces) KRAFT 2% Milk Shredded Reduced Fat Mozzarella Cheese

HEAT oven to 375°F. Spray 13×9-inch baking dish with no stick cooking spray.

MIX crumbles, pasta, spaghetti sauce and ½ cup Parmesan topping.

SPOON into prepared dish. Top with mozzarella cheese; sprinkle with remaining ¼ cup Parmesan topping.

BAKE 25 to 30 minutes.

Makes 8 servings

Tip: Add 1 box (10 ounces) chopped frozen spinach, thawed, well drained, to crumbles mixture before spooning into prepared baking dish.

Nutrition Information Per Serving: 430 calories, 13g total fat, 5g saturated fat, 25mg cholesterol, 1310mg sodium, 52g carbohydrate, 7g dietary fiber, 11g sugars, 26g protein

35% daily value vitamin A, 20% daily value vitamin C, 80% daily value calcium, 20% daily value iron

Exchange: 3 Starch, 2 Very Lean Meat, 2 Fat

MAIN DISHES

Cheesy Deluxe Primavera Mac Skillet

Prep: 5 minutes   Cook: 15 minutes

2⅓ cups water
1 package (14 ounces) KRAFT Light Deluxe Macaroni & Cheese Dinner
½ teaspoon dried basil leaves, crushed
½ teaspoon garlic powder
3 cups frozen vegetable medley (broccoli, cauliflower and carrots)

BRING water to boil in large skillet. Stir in Macaroni and seasonings; return to a boil.

STIR in vegetables. Reduce heat to medium-low; cover. Simmer 10 minutes or until macaroni is tender.

STIR in Cheese Sauce. Cook and stir 2 minutes on medium-high heat until thickened and creamy.

Makes 5 servings

Nutrition Information Per Serving (1 cup): 270 calories, 4g total fat, 2g saturated fat, 10mg cholesterol, 750mg sodium, 46g carbohydrate, 5g dietary fiber, 7g sugars, 13g protein

50% daily value vitamin A, 35% daily value vitamin C, 20% daily value calcium, 15% daily value iron

Exchange: 2½ Starch, 1 Vegetable, 1 Lean Meat

Salads & Sides Dishes

California Baked Potatoes

Prep: 10 minutes   Bake: 20 minutes

3 cold baked Idaho potatoes, cut into spears
½ cup KRAFT FREE CATALINA Fat Free Dressing
1 tablespoon garlic powder
1 tablespoon parsley flakes

HEAT oven to 375°F.

TOSS potato spears with dressing.

SPRINKLE each spear with garlic powder and parsley. Place on cookie sheet.

BAKE 20 minutes or until crispy.

Makes 6 servings

Nutrition Information Per Serving: 140 calories, 0g total fat, 0g saturated fat, 0mg cholesterol, 220mg sodium, 32g carbohydrate, 3g dietary fiber, 6g sugars, 3g protein

15% daily value vitamin A, 20% daily value vitamin C

Exchange: 2 Starch

Salads & Side Dishes

Apple Cranberry Mold
Prep: 10 minutes plus refrigerating

2 cups boiling apple juice
1 package (8-serving size) *or* 2 packages (4-serving size each) JELL-O Brand Cranberry Flavor Sugar Free Low Calorie Gelatin, *or* any red flavor
1½ cups reduced calorie cranberry juice cocktail

STIR boiling juice into gelatin in large bowl at least 2 minutes until completely dissolved. Stir in cranberry juice. Pour into 4-cup mold.

REFRIGERATE 4 hours or until firm. Unmold. Store leftover gelatin mold in refrigerator.

Makes 8 (½-cup) servings

How to Unmold: Dip mold in warm water for about 15 seconds. Gently pull gelatin from around edges with moist fingers. Place moistened serving plate on top of mold. Invert mold and plate; holding mold and plate together, shake slightly to loosen. Gently remove mold and center gelatin on plate.

Nutrition Information Per Serving: 45 calories, 0g total fat, 0g saturated fat, 0mg cholesterol, 80mg sodium, 10g carbohydrate, 0g dietary fiber, 9g sugars, 1g protein

15% daily value vitamin C

Exchange: ½ Fruit

Salads & Side Dishes

Cheesy Rice

Prep: 5 minutes   Cook: 10 minutes plus standing

2 cups water
2 cups MINUTE White Rice, uncooked
8 KRAFT 2% Milk Singles Cheese Food with Added Calcium

BRING water to boil. Stir in rice and 2% Milk Singles.

COOK and stir until 2% Milk Singles are melted; cover. Remove from heat. Let stand 5 to 7 minutes or until creamy. Stir.

Makes 6 (½-cup) servings

Special Extra: Add cooked carrots, broccoli or red and green peppers for a vegetable side dish.

Nutrition Information Per Serving: 180 calories, 4.5g total fat, 2.5g saturated fat, 15mg cholesterol, 400mg sodium, 26g carbohydrate, 0g dietary fiber, 2g sugars, 8g protein

15% daily value calcium

Exchange: 1½ Starch, 1 Meat

SALADS & SIDE DISHES

Crunchy Tuna Salad
Prep: 10 minutes

1 cup BREAKSTONE'S *or* KNUDSEN 2% Cottage Cheese
⅓ cup drained and flaked canned tuna in water
2 tablespoons chopped carrot
2 tablespoons chopped celery
2 tablespoons chopped onion
¼ teaspoon dill weed
⅛ teaspoon pepper
Tomato wedges and cucumber slices

MIX all ingredients except tomato and cucumber.

ARRANGE tuna mixture, tomato and cucumber on serving plates.

Makes 4 servings

Nutrition Information Per Serving: 130 calories, 2.5g total fat, 1.5g saturated fat, 25mg cholesterol, 490mg sodium, 6g carbohydrate, less than 1g dietary fiber, 4g sugars, 20g protein

60% daily value vitamin A

Exchange: 1 Vegetable, 3 Very Lean Meat

Salads & Side Dishes

Grilled Chicken Spinach Salad
Prep: 15 minutes

- 2 boneless skinless chicken breasts, grilled, cut into strips
- 5 cups torn spinach
- 1 cup sliced mushrooms
- ½ cup thinly sliced red onion wedges
- 4 slices OSCAR MAYER Bacon, crisply cooked, crumbled
- 1 cup KRAFT FREE CATALINA Fat Free Dressing

TOSS all ingredients except dressing in large bowl. Serve with dressing.

Makes 6 servings

Tip: Substitute grilled shrimp for grilled chicken.

Nutrition Information Per Serving: 180 calories, 4.5g total fat, 1.5g saturated fat, 55mg cholesterol, 590mg sodium, 13g carbohydrate, 2g dietary fiber, 10g sugars, 21g protein

70% daily value vitamin A, 15% daily value vitamin C, 10% daily value iron

Exchange: 1 Carbohydrate, 2 Lean Meat

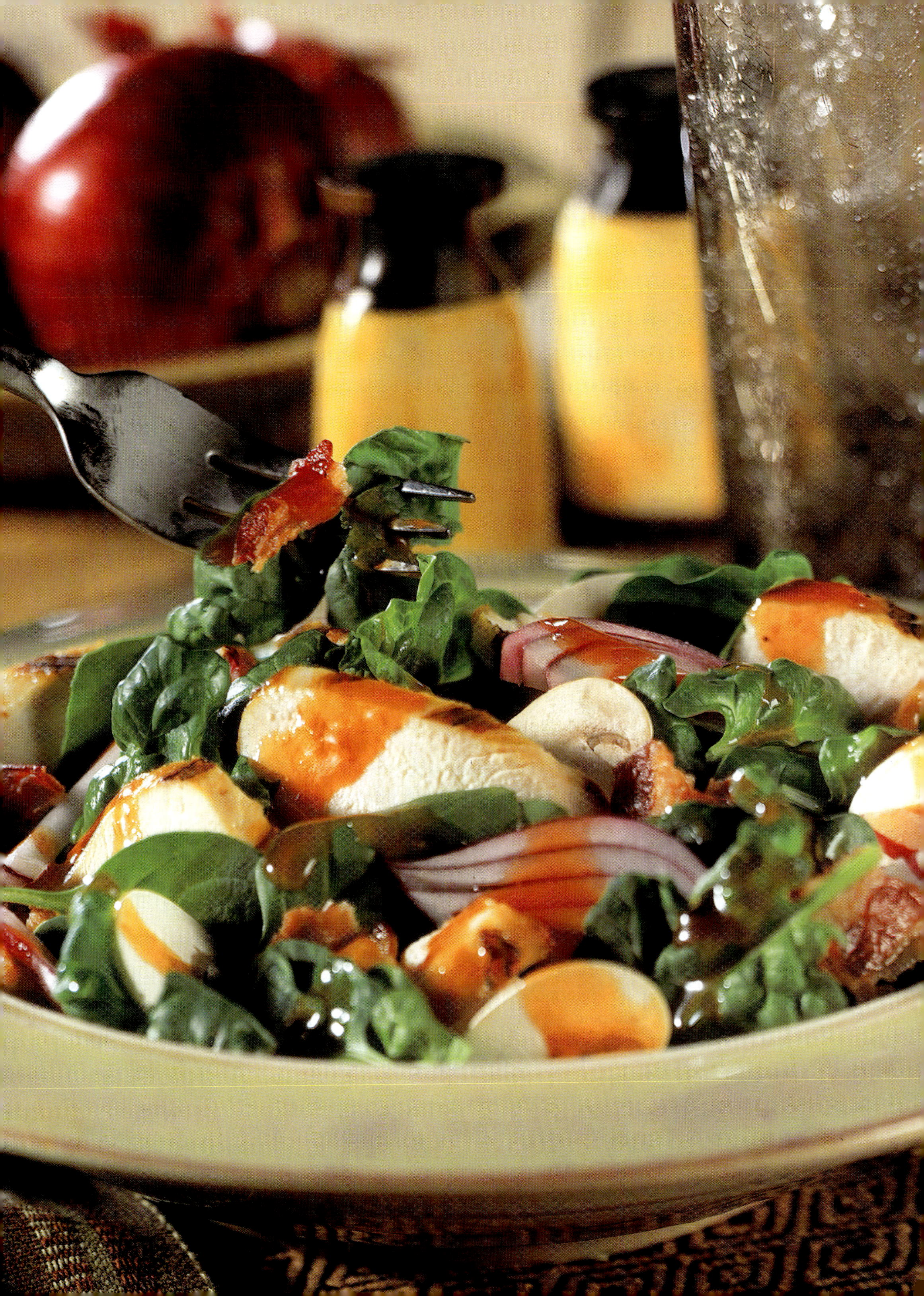

SALADS & SIDE DISHES

Cottage Cheese Zucchini Casserole

Prep: 20 minutes   Bake: 45 minutes

2 pounds zucchini, sliced
1 cup chopped onions
1 cup sliced mushrooms
1 clove garlic, minced
2 tablespoons oil
1 container (16 ounces) BREAKSTONE'S or KNUDSEN 2% Cottage Cheese, any variety
2 cups KRAFT Shredded Sharp Cheddar Cheese
3 eggs, beaten
2 tablespoons flour
2 tablespoons Italian seasoning
½ teaspoon salt

HEAT oven to 350°F. Grease 2½-quart casserole.

COOK and stir zucchini, onions, mushrooms and garlic in oil in large skillet on medium-high heat 5 minutes. Drain in a colander; set aside. Mix remaining ingredients in large bowl. Stir in vegetable mixture. Pour into prepared casserole.

BAKE 45 minutes or until knife inserted in center comes out clean.

Makes 10 servings

Nutrition Information Per Serving: 190 calories, 13g total fat, 6g saturated fat, 90mg cholesterol, 420mg sodium, 9g carbohydrate, 2g dietary fiber, 3g sugars, 13g protein

15% daily value vitamin A, 10% daily value vitamin C, 20% daily value calcium

Exchange: 1 Vegetable, 2 Medium Fat Meat

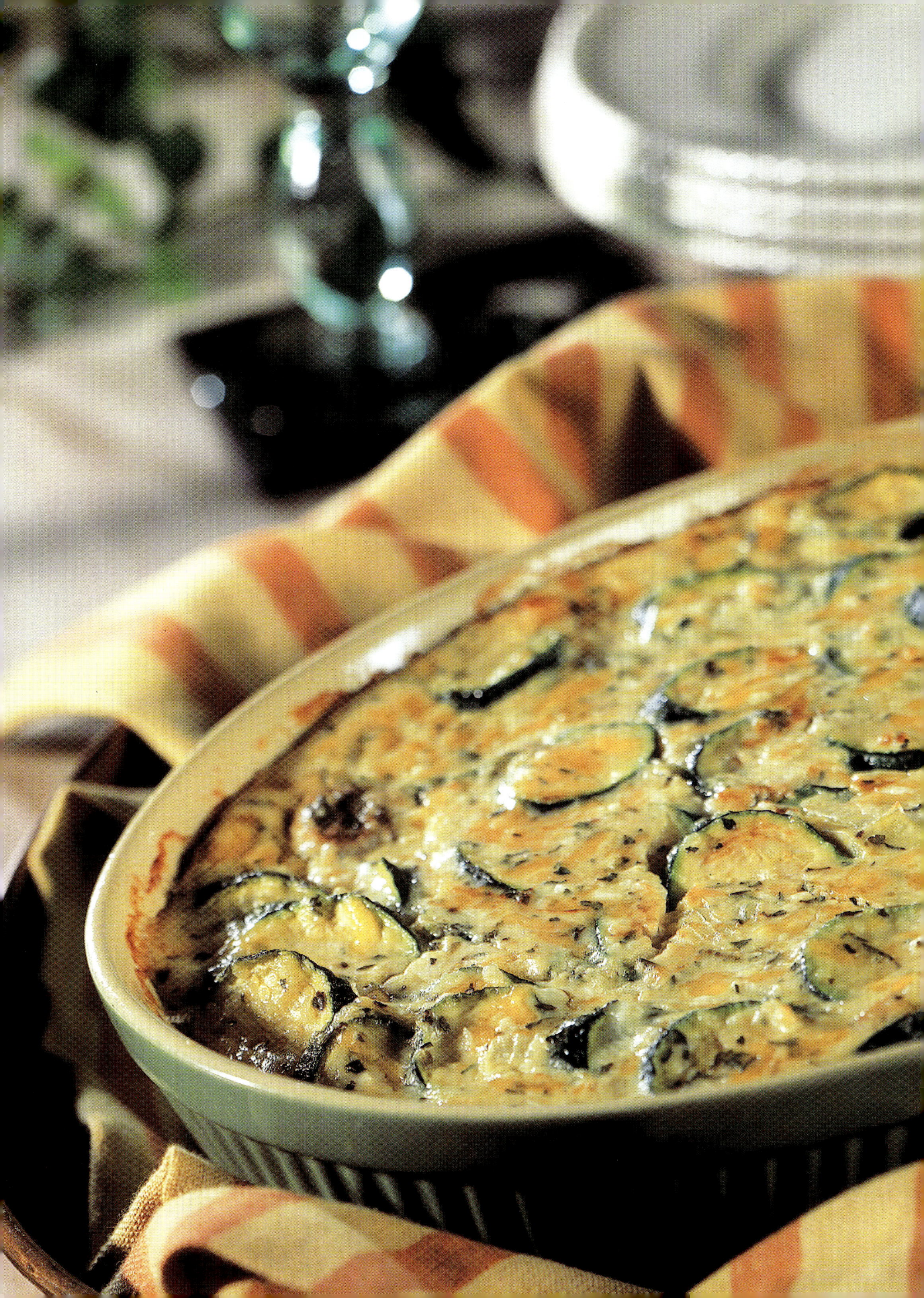

Salads & Side Dishes

Fresh Garden Spinach Salad
Prep: 15 minutes

5 cups torn romaine lettuce
4 cups torn spinach
1 can (15 ounces) red kidney beans, rinsed, drained
1 cup broccoli flowerets
1 cup sliced carrots
1 red *or* green pepper, cut into thin strips
1 tomato, cut into wedges
¼ cup slivered red onion
¾ cup KRAFT LIGHT DONE RIGHT! Italian Dressing

TOSS vegetables and dressing in large bowl.

Makes 6 servings

Nutrition Information Per Serving: 150 calories, 5g total fat, 0g saturated fat, 0mg cholesterol, 280mg sodium, 21g carbohydrate, 7g dietary fiber, 7g sugars, 7g protein

100% daily value vitamin A, 100% daily value vitamin C, 10% daily value calcium, 20% daily value iron

Exchange: 1 Starch, 1 Vegetable, 1 Fat

SALADS & SIDE DISHES

Tuscan Vegetable Potato Salad

Prep: 10 minutes plus refrigerating   Microwave: 22 minutes

2 pounds small new potatoes, quartered (about 6 cups)
¼ cup water
½ pound green beans, cut into 2-inch pieces
½ pound carrots, diagonally sliced
1 small red onion, cut into wedges
1 cup KRAFT LIGHT DONE RIGHT! Italian Reduced Fat Dressing

PLACE potatoes and water in 3-quart microwavable casserole; cover. Microwave on HIGH 10 minutes.

ADD remaining vegetables. Microwave 10 to 12 minutes or until vegetables are tender. Drain.

TOSS vegetables and dressing. Refrigerate several hours. Sprinkle with grated Parmesan cheese, if desired.

Makes 8 servings

Nutrition Information Per Serving: 150 calories, 4.5g total fat, 0g saturated fat, 0mg cholesterol, 250mg sodium, 22g carbohydrate, 4g dietary fiber, 5g sugars, 4g protein

100% daily value vitamin A, 25% daily value vitamin C, 20% daily value iron

Exchange: 1 Starch, 1 Vegetable, 1 Fat

Salads & Side Dishes

Creamy Mexican Mold
Prep: 10 minutes   Refrigerate: 4 hours

1 jar (20 ounces) TACO BELL® HOME ORIGINALS® Thick 'N Chunky Salsa
1 cup BREAKSTONE'S Light Sour Cream
⅓ cup chopped ripe olives
⅓ cup sliced green onions
1 teaspoon hot pepper sauce
2 envelopes KNOX Unflavored Gelatine
⅔ cup tomato juice
Baked tortilla chips or assorted cut-up vegetables

MIX salsa, sour cream, olives, green onions and hot pepper sauce in medium bowl; set aside.

SPRINKLE gelatine over tomato juice in small saucepan; let stand 1 minute. Stir gelatine on low heat until completely dissolved, about 3 minutes. Stir gelatine mixture into salsa mixture. Pour into 4-cup mold.

REFRIGERATE 4 hours or until firm. Unmold onto serving dish. Refrigerate until ready to serve. Serve with baked tortilla chips or assorted cut-up vegetables, if desired.

Makes 3¾ cups spread or 30 (2-tablespoon) servings

Nutrition Information Per Serving (2 tablespoons): 25 calories, 1g total fat, 0.5g saturated fat, less than 5mg cholesterol, 190mg sodium, 2g carbohydrate, 0g dietary fiber, 2g sugars, 1g protein

Exchange: FREE

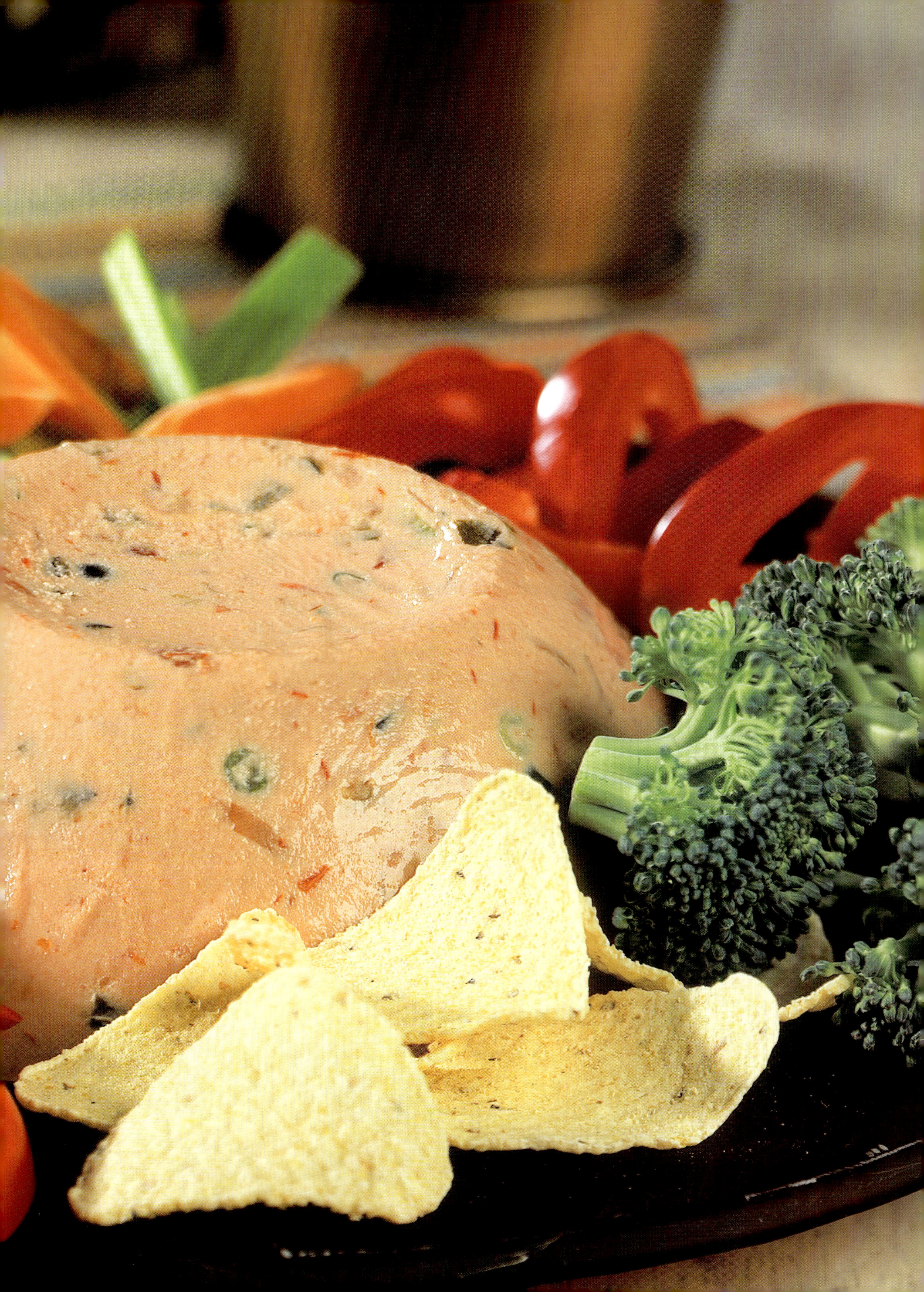

Desserts

Shredded Wheat Autumn Crisp

Prep: 20 minutes   Bake: 45 minutes

5 cups peeled, cored and sliced apples
½ cup firmly packed light brown sugar, divided
1 tablespoon lemon juice
1 tablespoon MINUTE Tapioca
¼ teaspoon ground cinnamon
1½ cups POST SPOON SIZE Shredded Wheat Cereal, finely crushed
¼ cup (4 tablespoons) margarine, melted

HEAT oven to 350°F. Mix apples, ¼ cup of the sugar, lemon juice, tapioca and cinnamon in large bowl. Let stand 10 minutes. Meanwhile stir crushed cereal, remaining ¼ cup sugar and margarine in medium bowl until well mixed.

SPREAD apple mixture in ungreased 1½-quart baking dish. Sprinkle evenly with cereal topping.

BAKE 45 minutes or until topping is browned and apples are tender when pierced with fork.

Makes 6 servings

Nutrition Information Per Serving: 240 calories, 8g total fat, 1.5g saturated fat, 0mg cholesterol, 95mg sodium, 43g carbohydrate, 3g dietary fiber, 29g sugars, 2g protein

Exchange: 2 Fruit, 1 Carbohydrate, 1½ Fat

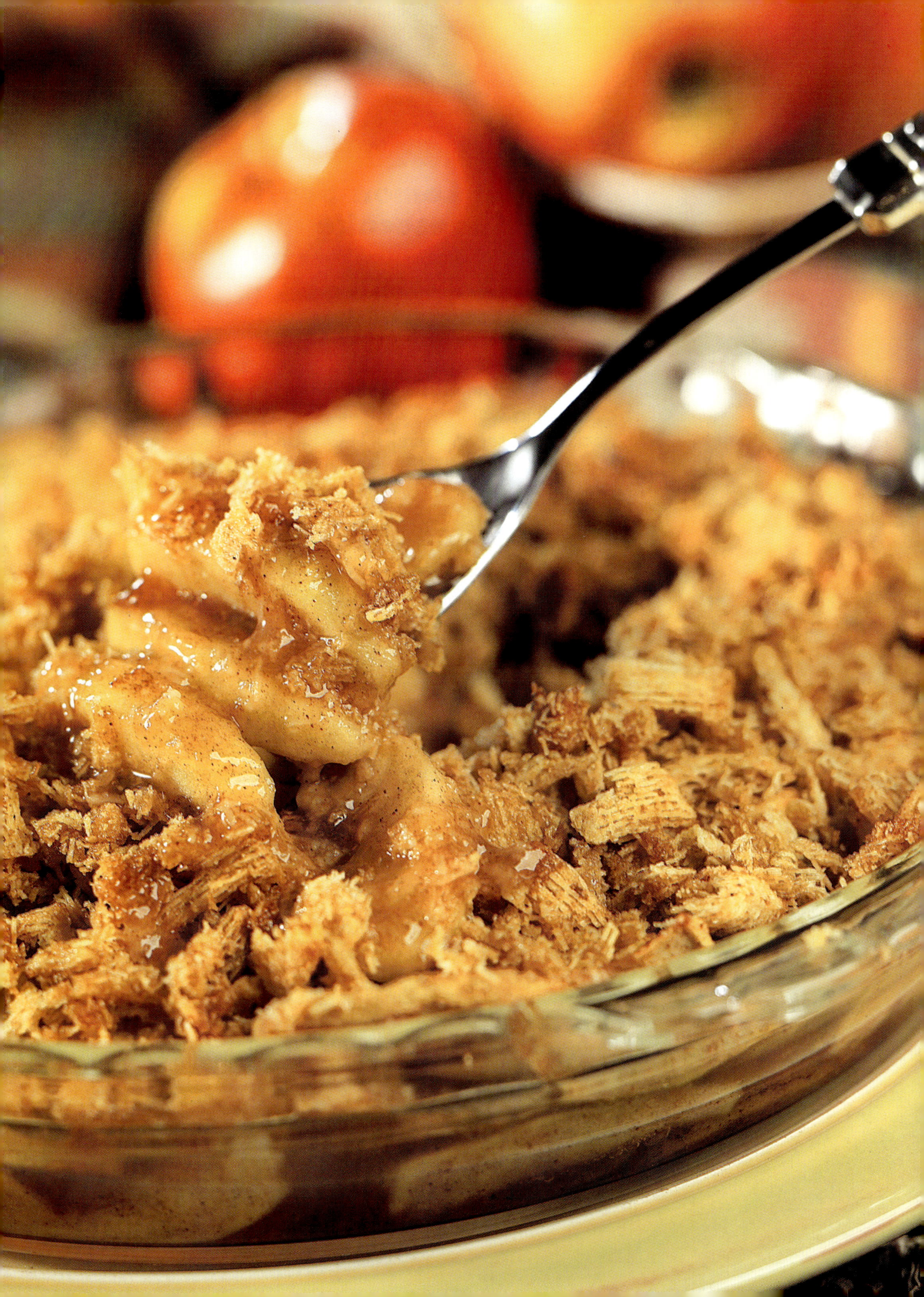

Desserts

Low Fat Lemon Soufflé Cheesecake

Prep: 15 minutes plus refrigerating

1 graham cracker, crushed, divided
⅔ cup boiling water
1 package (4-serving size) JELL-O Brand Lemon Flavor Sugar Free Low Calorie Gelatin Dessert
1 cup BREAKSTONE'S *or* KNUDSEN 2% Cottage Cheese
1 container (8 ounces) PHILADELPHIA FREE Fat Free Cream Cheese
2 cups thawed COOL WHIP FREE Whipped Topping

SPRINKLE ½ of the crumbs onto side of 8- or 9-inch springform pan or 9-inch pie plate which has been sprayed with no stick cooking spray.

STIR boiling water into gelatin in large bowl at least 2 minutes until completely dissolved. Pour into blender container. Add cheeses; cover. Blend on medium speed until smooth, scraping down sides occasionally.

POUR into large bowl. Gently stir in whipped topping. Pour into prepared pan; smooth top. Sprinkle remaining crumbs around outside edge.

REFRIGERATE 4 hours or until set. Remove side of pan just before serving. Store leftover cheesecake in refrigerator.

Makes 8 servings

Nutrition Information Per Serving: 100 calories, 2g total fat, 1.5g saturated fat, 10mg cholesterol, 300mg sodium, 11g carbohydrate, 0g dietary fiber, 5g sugars, 9g protein

10% daily value calcium

Exchange: 1 Starch, ½ Very Lean Meat

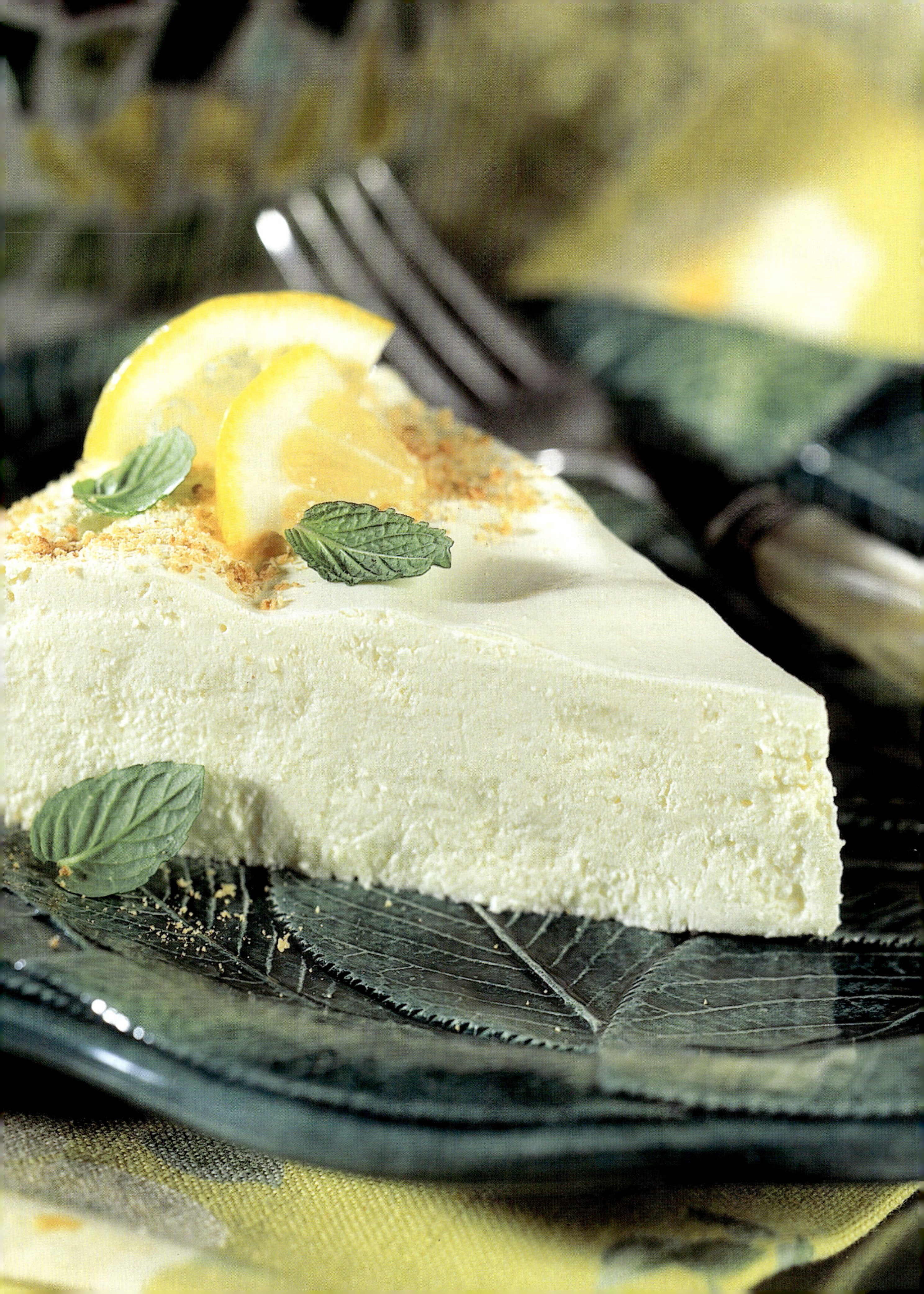

DESSERTS

Boo Cups
Prep: 15 minutes

3¼ cups cold fat free milk
2 packages (4-serving size each) JELL-O Chocolate Flavor Fat Free Sugar Free Instant Reduced Calorie Pudding & Pie Filling
1 tub (8 ounces) COOL WHIP FREE Whipped Topping, thawed, divided
1 package (7¾ ounces) SNACKWELL'S Chocolate Sandwich Cookies, crushed, divided

POUR milk into large bowl. Add pudding mixes. Beat with wire whisk 1 minute. Gently stir in ½ of the whipped topping and ½ of the crushed cookies.

SPOON 1 tablespoon crushed cookies into 10 individual cups. Evenly divide the pudding mixture among the cups. Top with remaining crushed cookies.

DROP remaining whipped topping by spoonfuls onto desserts to create "ghosts." Refrigerate until ready to serve. Store leftover dessert in refrigerator.

Makes 10 (½-cup) servings

Nutrition Information Per Serving: 190 calories, 4g total fat, 2g saturated fat, 0mg cholesterol, 480mg sodium, 36g carbohydrate, 1g dietary fiber, 16g sugars, 4g protein

10% daily value calcium

Exchange: 2 Carbohydrate, 1 Fat

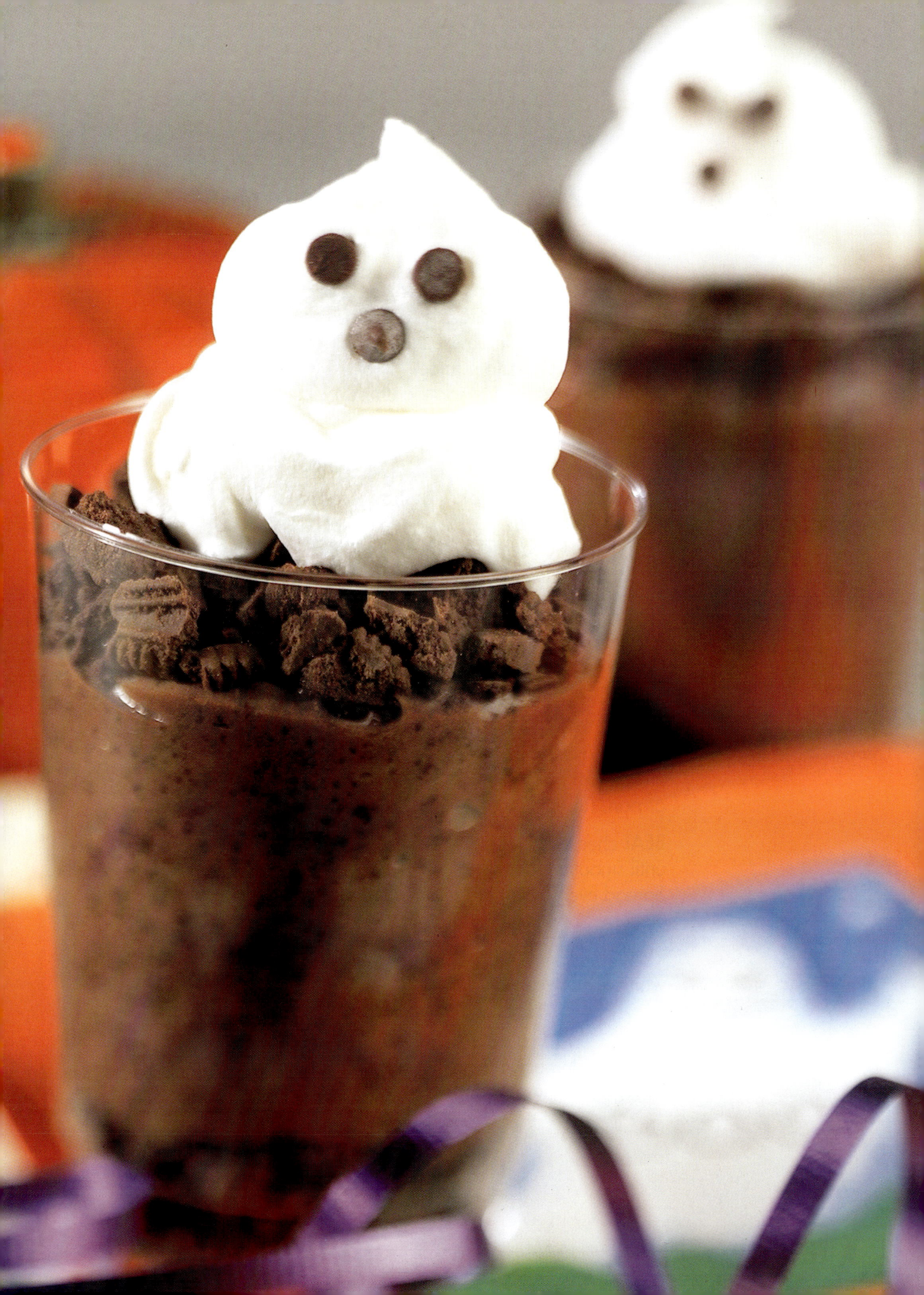

Desserts

Peach Melba Dessert
Prep: 15 minutes plus refrigerating

1½ cups boiling water
1 package (8-serving size) *or* 2 pkg. (4-serving size each) JELL-O Brand Raspberry Flavor Sugar Free Low Calorie Gelatin
2 cups cold apple juice
1½ cups graham cracker crumbs
½ cup sugar, divided
½ cup (1 stick) margarine, melted
1 package (8 ounces) PHILADELPHIA Neufchatel Cheese, ⅓ Less Fat than Cream Cheese, softened
1 tub (8 ounces) COOL WHIP FREE Whipped Topping, thawed, divided
1 can (16 ounces) sliced peaches, drained
1 cup raspberries

STIR boiling water into gelatin in large bowl at least 2 minutes until completely dissolved. Stir in apple juice. Refrigerate about 1½ hours or until thickened.

MEANWHILE mix crumbs, ¼ cup of the sugar and margarine in 13×9-inch pan. Press firmly onto bottom of pan. Refrigerate until ready to fill.

BEAT cheese and remaining ¼ cup sugar in large bowl until smooth. Gently stir in 2 cups of the whipped topping. Spread evenly over crust. Arrange fruits on cheese mixture. Spoon gelatin over cheese layer.

REFRIGERATE 3 hours or until firm. Serve with remaining whipped topping.

Makes 15 servings

Nutrition Information Per Serving: 210 calories, 11g total fat, 4.5g saturated fat, 10mg cholesterol, 220mg sodium,

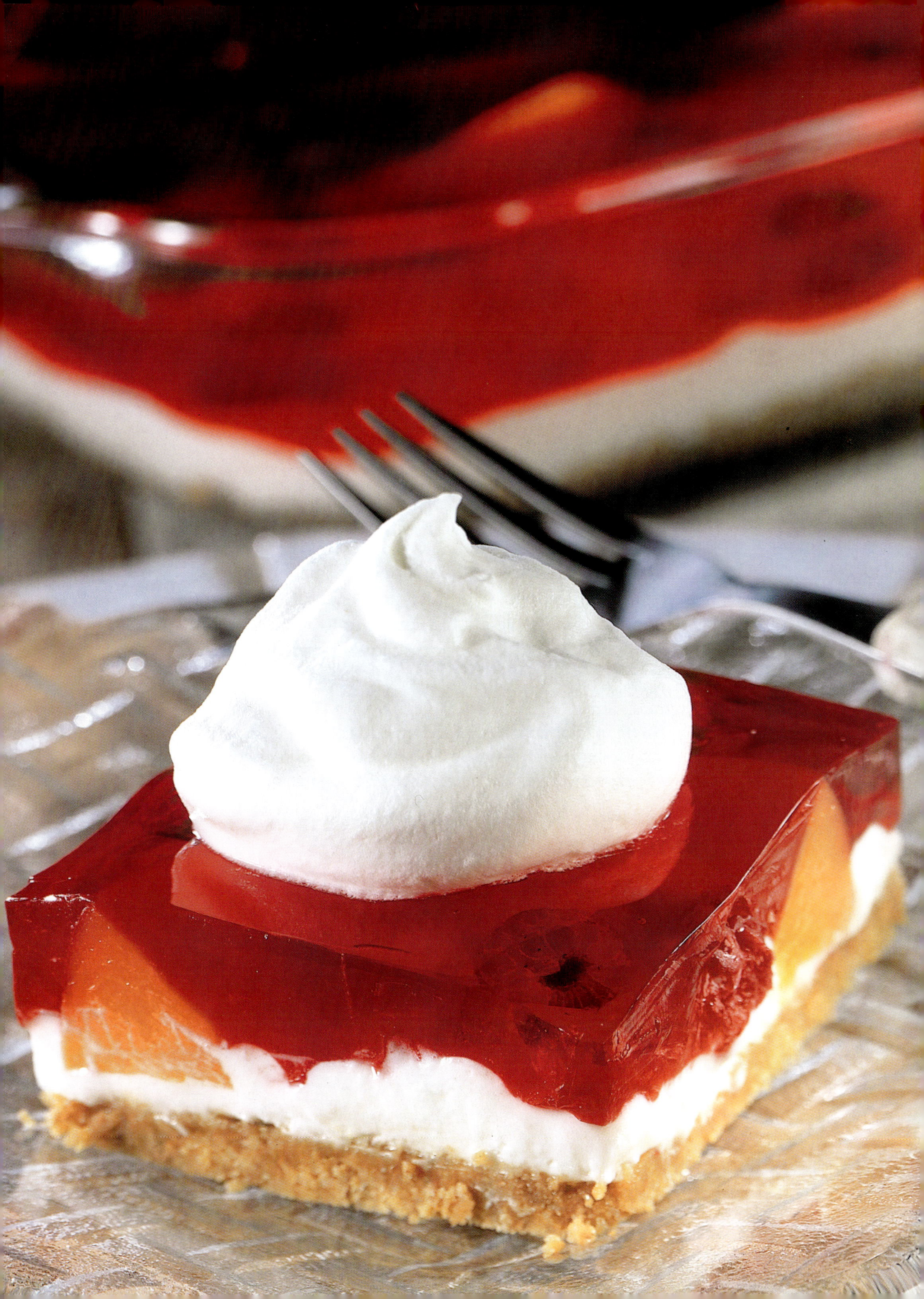

DESSERTS

Yogurt Crunch Parfaits
Prep: 5 minutes

SODIUM

1 container (8 ounces) BREYERS Lowfat Yogurt, any flavor
1 tub (8 ounces) COOL WHIP FREE Whipped Topping, thawed, divided
1 banana, sliced
1 can (20 ounces) pineapple chunks, drained
1 cup POST SELECTS BANANA NUT CRUNCH Cereal

STIR yogurt and ½ of the whipped topping in large bowl until smooth. Alternately layer yogurt mixture, banana, pineapple chunks, cereal and remaining whipped topping in 6 parfait glasses; repeat layers.

Makes 6 servings

Nutrition Information Per Serving: 220 calories, 3.5g total fat, 2.5g saturated fat, less than 5mg cholesterol, 80mg sodium, 48g carbohydrate, 2g dietary fiber, 29g sugars, 3g protein

15% daily value vitamin C, 15% daily value iron

Exchange: 3 Carbohydrate

Desserts

Café Pudding

Prep: 5 minutes

2 cups cold fat free milk
1 package (4-serving size) JELL-O Vanilla Flavor Fat Free Sugar Free Reduced Calorie Instant Pudding & Pie Filling
¼ cup GENERAL FOODS INTERNATIONAL COFFEES Sugar Free Fat Free, French Vanilla Café Flavor

POUR milk into medium bowl. Add pudding mix and flavored instant coffee. Beat with whisk 2 minutes. Spoon pudding mixture into 4 dessert glasses. Refrigerate until ready to serve.

Makes 4 (½-cup) servings

Nutrition Information Per Serving: 90 calories, 0.5g total fat, 0g saturated fat, less than 5mg cholesterol, 440mg sodium, 16g carbohydrate, 0g dietary fiber, 6g sugars, 4g protein

15% daily value calcium

Exchange: 1 Carbohydrate

DESSERTS

Double Chocolate Bread Pudding

Prep: 15 minutes   Bake: 40 minutes plus standing

- 5 cups fat free milk
- 2 packages (4-serving size each) JELL-O Chocolate Flavor Sugar Free Cook and Serve Pudding & Pie Filling
- 5 cups French bread cubes
- 1 package (4 ounces) BAKER'S GERMAN'S Sweet Chocolate, chopped

HEAT oven to 350°F.

POUR cold milk into large bowl. Add pudding mixes. Beat with wire whisk 1 minute until well blended. Stir in bread. Pour pudding mixture into 13×9-inch baking dish. Sprinkle evenly with chopped chocolate.

BAKE 40 minutes or until pudding just comes to a boil in the center. Remove from oven. Let stand 10 minutes before serving. Serve warm. Store leftover pudding in refrigerator.

Makes 12 servings

Dalmatian Bread Pudding: Substitute JELL-O Vanilla Flavor Sugar Free Cook and Serve Pudding & Pie Filling for Chocolate Flavor Pudding to create a delicious black and white bread pudding.

Nutrition Information Per Serving: 150 calories, 3.5g total fat, 2g saturated fat, less than 5mg cholesterol, 230mg sodium, 26g carbohydrate, 2g dietary fiber, 10g sugars, 6g protein

15% daily value calcium, 10% daily value iron

Exchange: 2 Carbohydrate, ½ Low Fat Milk

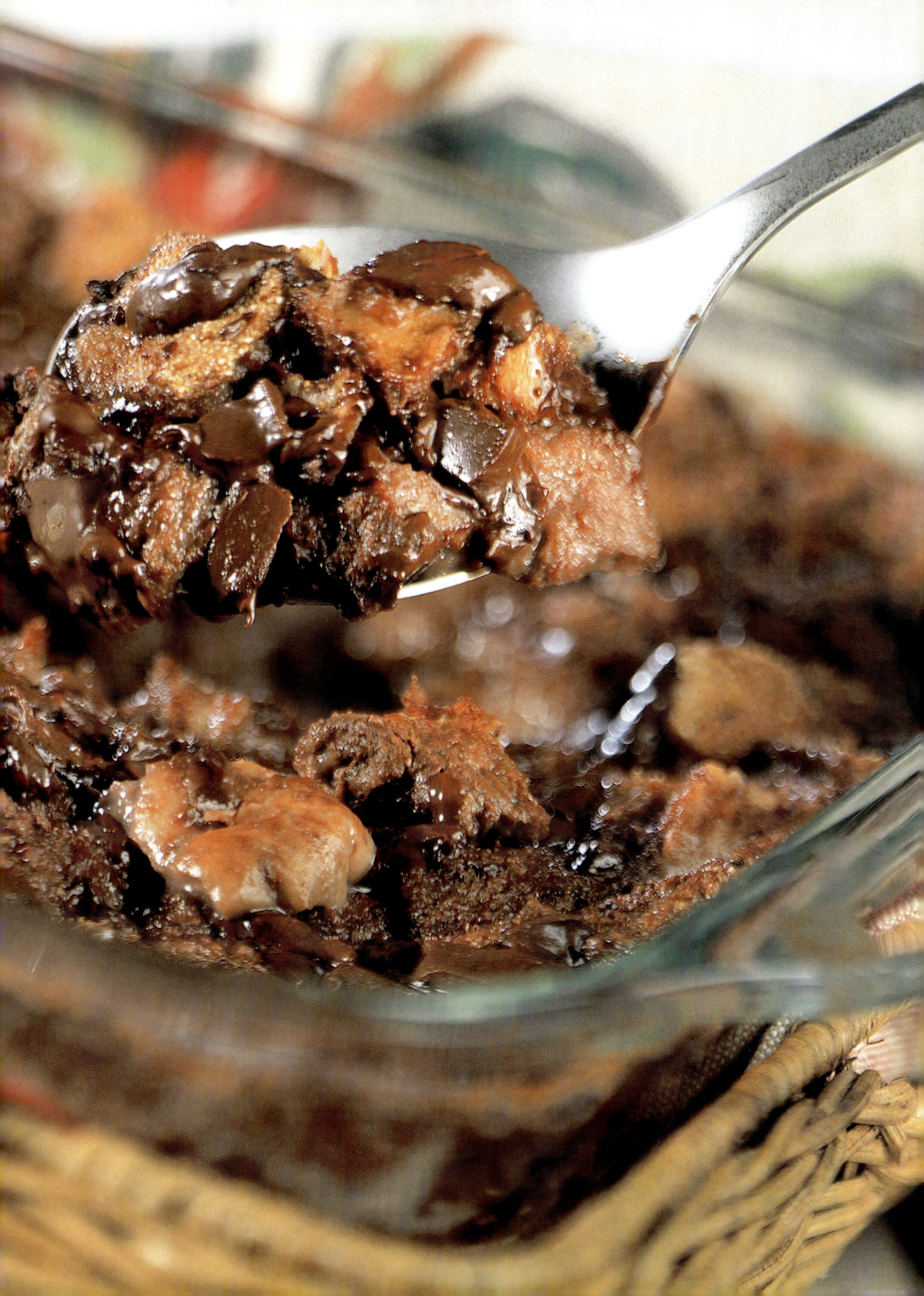

Desserts

Paradise Parfaits
Prep: 10 minutes

¼ cup GENERAL FOODS INTERNATIONAL COFFEES Fat Free Sugar Free, French Vanilla Café Flavor
1 tablespoon hot water
2 cups cold fat free milk
1 package (4-serving size) JELL-O Vanilla Flavor Fat Free Sugar Free Instant Reduced Calorie Pudding & Pie Filling
1 cup thawed COOL WHIP FREE Fat Free Whipped Topping
1½ cups assorted fresh fruit, such as sliced strawberries, raspberries, chopped peaches *or* crushed pineapple

DISSOLVE flavored instant coffee in hot water in medium bowl. Pour milk into coffee mixture. Add pudding mix. Beat with wire whisk 2 minutes. Gently stir in whipped topping.

SPOON ½ of the pudding mixture into 6 dessert glasses. Layer with fruit. Spoon remaining pudding mixture over fruit.

REFRIGERATE until ready to serve. Garnish with additional whipped topping and fruit, if desired.

Makes 6 servings

Nutrition Information Per Serving: 90 calories, 1g total fat, 1g saturated fat, 0mg cholesterol, 300mg sodium, 18g carbohydrate, 1g dietary fiber, 8g sugars, 3g protein

40% daily value vitamin C, 10% daily value calcium

Exchange: 1 Carbohydrate

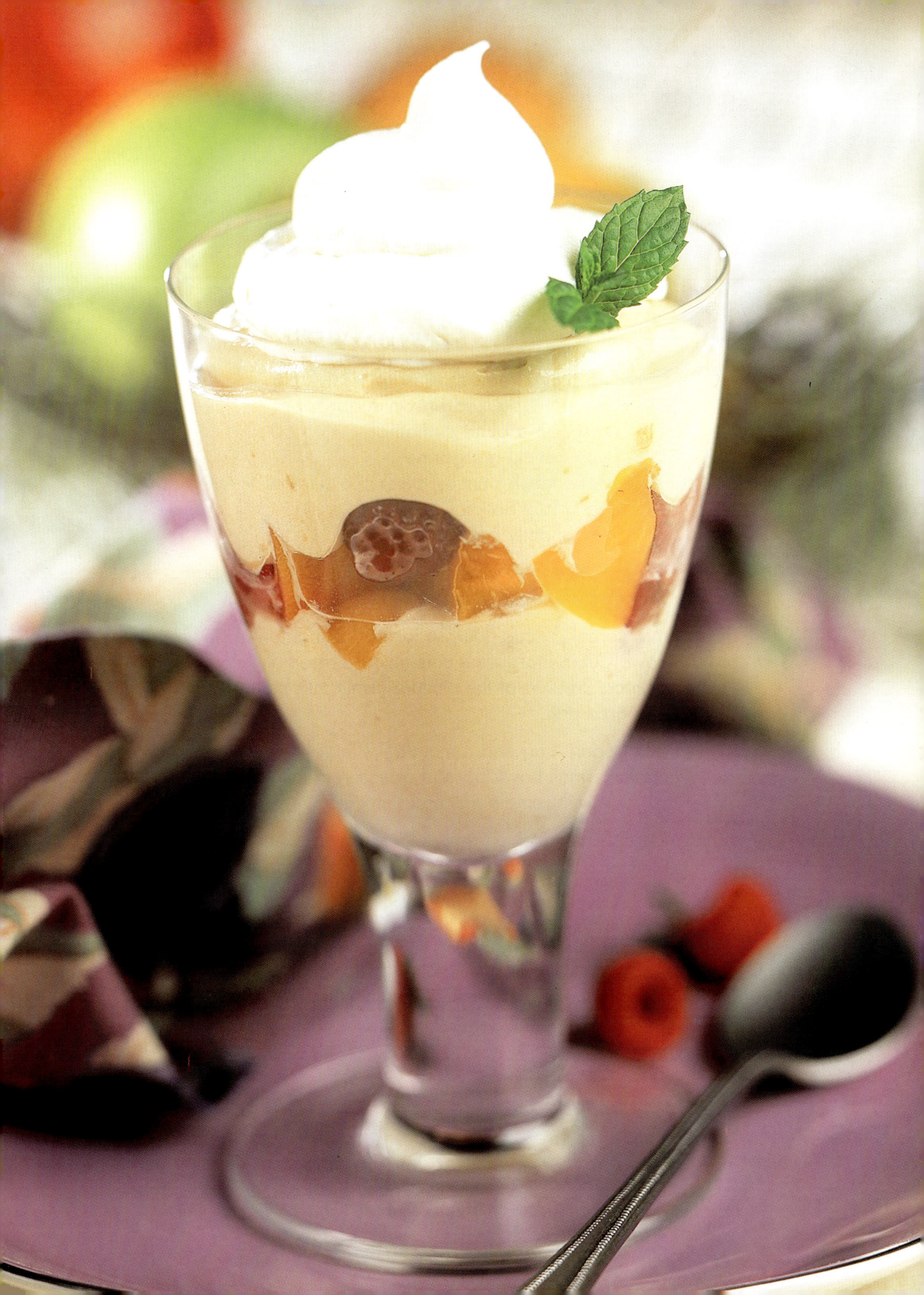

DESSERTS

Cereal Yogurt Bars
Prep: 15 minutes   Bake: 30 minutes

SODIUM

2 cups POST Raisin Bran Cereal
¾ cup plus 2 tablespoons flour, divided
¼ cup firmly packed brown sugar
½ teaspoon ground cinnamon
½ cup (1 stick) margarine
1 container (8 ounces) BREYERS® Lowfat Yogurt, any fruit flavor
1 egg, slightly beaten

HEAT oven to 350°F. Spray 8-inch square baking pan with no stick cooking spray.

MIX cereal, ¾ cup flour, sugar and cinnamon in small bowl. Cut in margarine until mixture resembles coarse crumbs. Press ½ of the mixture firmly into bottom of prepared pan.

MIX yogurt, egg and remaining 2 tablespoons flour in another small bowl. Spread over cereal mixture in pan; sprinkle with remaining cereal mixture.

BAKE 30 minutes or until golden brown. Cool in pan on wire rack. Cut into bars.

Makes 16 bars

Nutrition Information Per Bar: 130 calories, 6g total fat, 1.5g saturated fat, 15mg cholesterol, 125mg sodium, 17g carbohydrate, 1g dietary fiber, 8g sugars, 2g protein

10% daily value iron

Exchange: 1 Starch, 1 Fat

DESSERTS

Chocolate Banana Split
Prep: 15 minutes

FAT

2 cups cold fat free milk
1 package (4-serving size) JELL-O Chocolate Flavor Fat Free Sugar Free Instant Reduced Calorie Pudding & Pie Filling
2 medium bananas, sliced
½ cup thawed COOL WHIP LITE Whipped Topping
1 tablespoon chopped walnuts

POUR milk into medium bowl. Add pudding mix. Beat with wire whisk 2 minutes.

SPOON ½ of the pudding evenly into 4 dessert dishes. Layer with banana slices. Spoon remaining pudding over bananas.

REFRIGERATE until ready to serve. Top each serving with 2 tablespoons whipped topping. Sprinkle with walnuts.

Makes 4 (1-cup) servings

Nutrition Information Per Serving: 160 calories, 3g total fat, 1.5g saturated fat, less than 5mg cholesterol, 380mg sodium, 30g carbohydrate, 2g dietary fiber, 17g sugars, 6g protein

10% daily value vitamin C, 15% daily value calcium

Exchange: 2 Carbohydrate, ½ Fat

DESSERTS

Easy Tiramisu

Prep: 15 minutes

1 package (8 ounces) PHILADELPHIA FREE Fat Free Cream Cheese, softened
½ cup cooled brewed MAXWELL HOUSE Coffee, divided
1 tablespoon powdered sugar
½ teaspoon vanilla
1 tub (8 ounces) COOL WHIP FREE Whipped Topping, thawed, divided
10 SNACKWELL'S Sugar Free Shortbread Cookies, divided

BEAT cream cheese, ¼ cup coffee, sugar and vanilla in medium bowl with electric mixer at medium speed until creamy. Gently stir in 2 cups whipped topping.

SPOON about 1 cup cheese mixture into bottom of 1-quart bowl. Dip 5 cookies in remaining ¼ cup coffee for 5 seconds; evenly arrange on cheese. Repeat layers once; spread with remaining cheese mixture and remaining whipped topping.

REFRIGERATE 1 hour or until ready to serve. Sift cocoa over dessert, if desired.

Makes 8 (½-cup) servings

Nutrition Information Per Serving: 140 calories, 4g total fat, 2g saturated fat, 10mg cholesterol, 230mg sodium, 22g carbohydrate, 0g dietary fiber, 6g sugars, 5g protein

15% daily value vitamin A, 10% daily value calcium

Exchange: 1½ Carbohydrate, 1 Fat

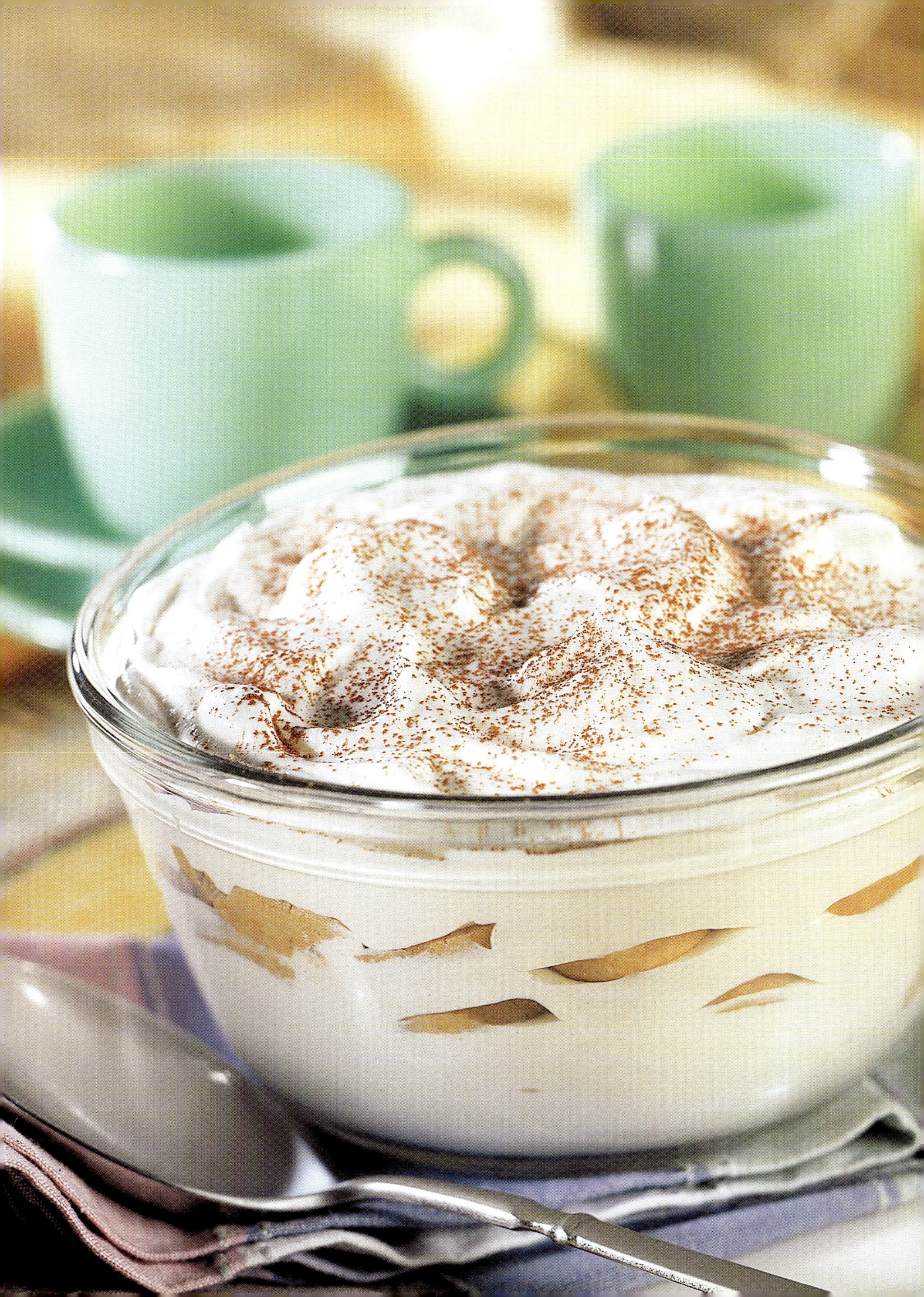

Desserts

Peanut Butter and Jam Parfaits

Prep: 10 minutes

2 cups cold fat free milk
1 package (4-serving size) JELL-O Vanilla Flavor Fat Free Sugar Free Instant Reduced Calorie Pudding & Pie Filling
3 tablespoons peanut butter
½ teaspoon water
¼ cup fruit juice sweetened raspberry preserves

POUR cold milk into large bowl. Add pudding mix. Beat with wire whisk 1 minute until smooth. Add peanut butter and continue beating with whisk until completely incorporated.

STIR water into preserves. Spoon about ¼ cup pudding mixture into each of 4 dessert glasses. Top with ½ of the preserves. Repeat layers. Top with additional preserves, if desired.

REFRIGERATE until ready to serve. Store leftover dessert in refrigerator.

Makes 4 servings

Nutrition Information Per Serving: 180 calories, 6g total fat, 1.5g saturated fat, less than 5mg cholesterol, 460mg sodium, 27g carbohydrate, less than 1g dietary fiber, 18g sugars, 7g protein

15% daily value calcium

Exchange: 2 Carbohydrate, 1 Fat

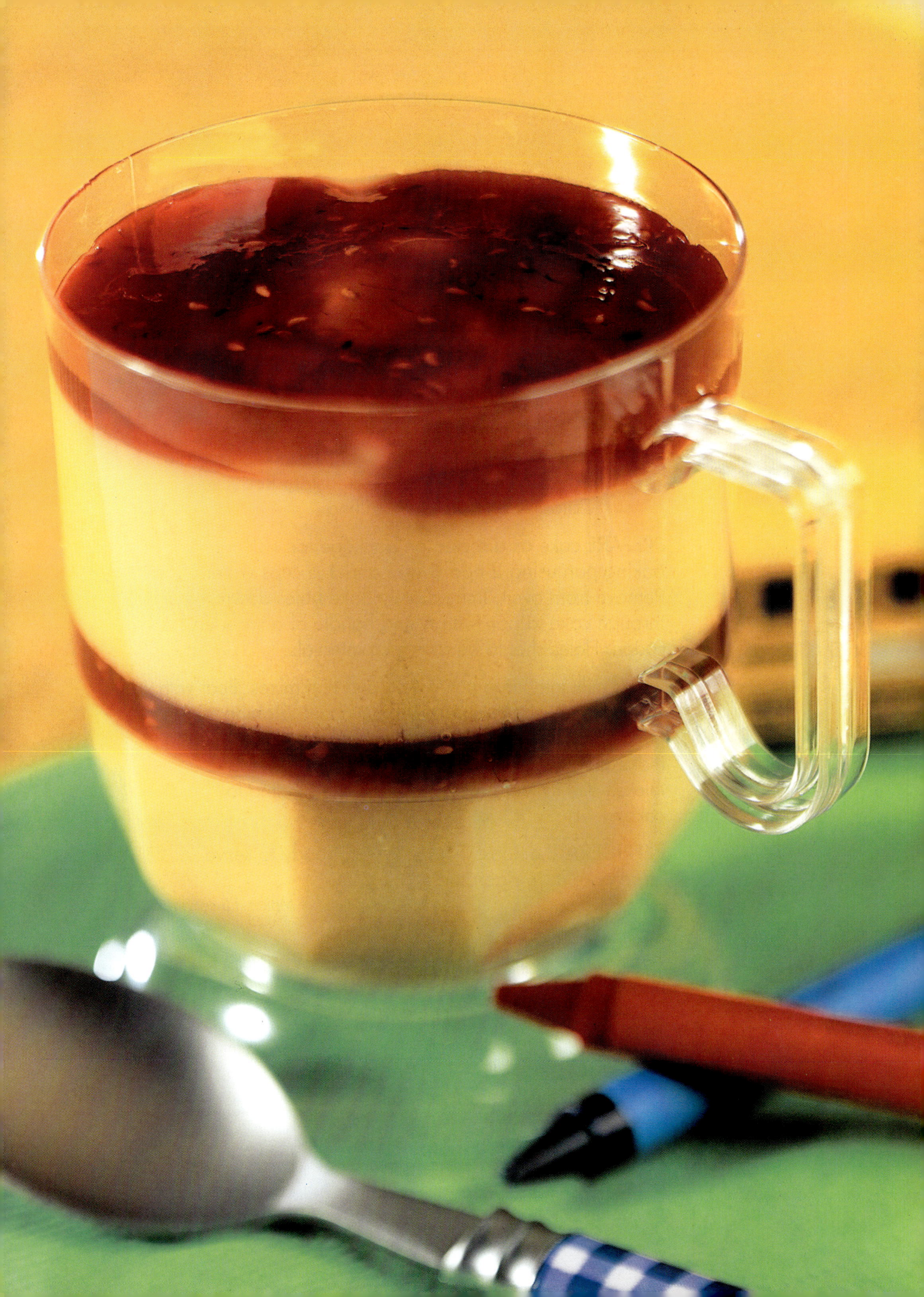

DESSERTS

Chocolate Pudding Poke Cake
Prep: 30 minutes plus refrigerating

1 package (2-layer size) white cake mix
2 egg whites
1⅓ cups water
4 cups cold fat free milk
2 packages (4-serving size each) JELL-O Chocolate Flavor Fat Free Sugar Free Instant Reduced Calorie Pudding & Pie Filling

PREPARE cake as directed on package for 13×9-inch baking pan using 2 egg whites and 1⅓ cups water. Remove from oven. Immediately poke holes down through cake to pan with round handle of a wooden spoon. Holes should be at 1-inch intervals.

POUR milk into large bowl. Add pudding mixes. Beat with wire whisk 2 minutes. Quickly pour about ½ of the thin pudding mixture evenly over warm cake and into holes to make stripes. Let remaining pudding mixture stand to thicken slightly. Spoon over top of cake, swirling to "frost" cake.

REFRIGERATE at least 1 hour or until ready to serve. Store cake in refrigerator.

Makes 15 servings

Nutrition Information Per Serving: 190 calories, 4g total fat, 0.5g saturated fat, 0mg cholesterol, 440mg sodium, 35g carbohydrate, less than 1g dietary fiber, 26g sugars, 5g protein

15% daily value calcium

Exchange: 2 Carbohydrate, ½ Fat

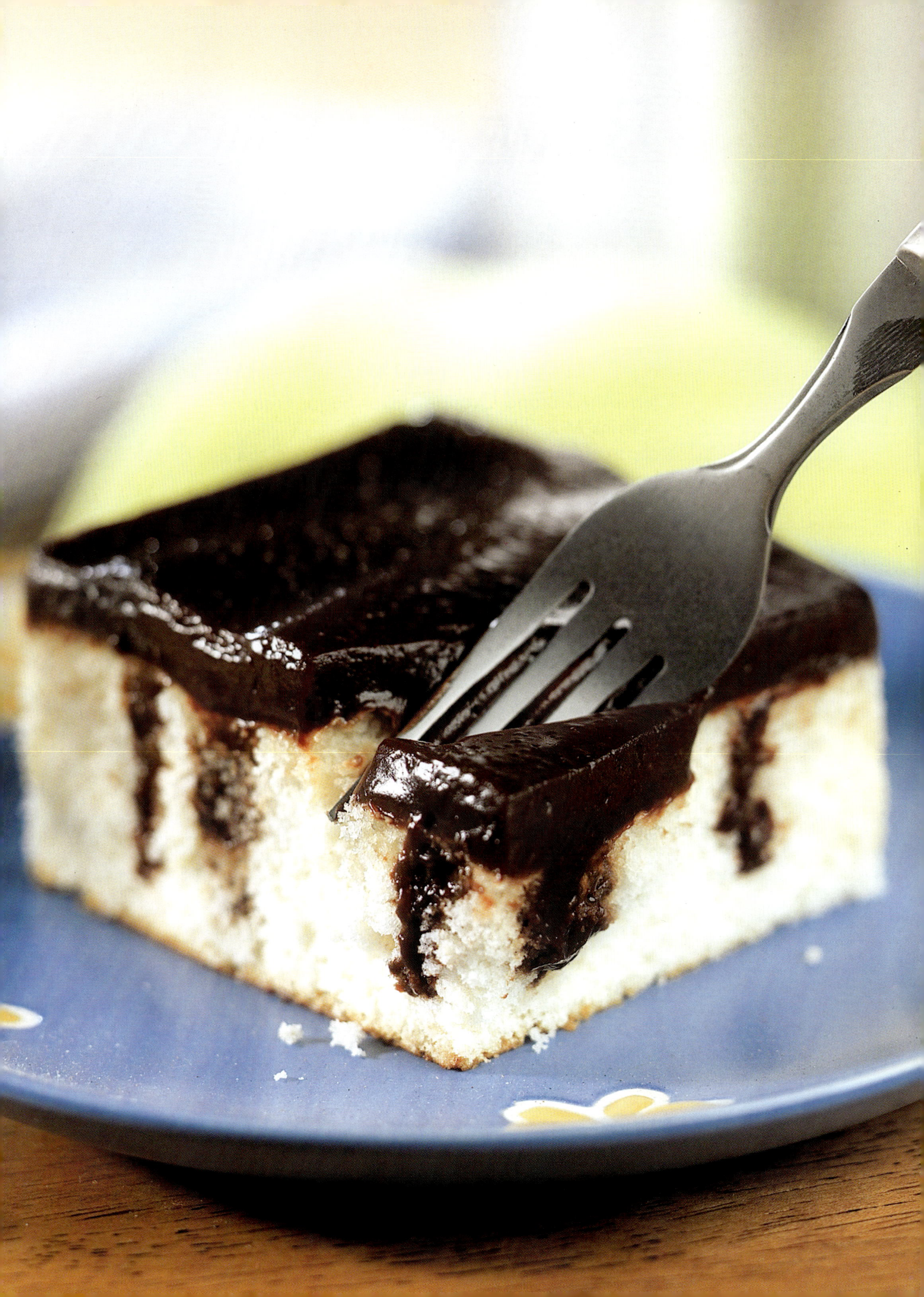

BEVERAGES

Sunset Punch

Prep: 5 minutes

CALORIE   SODIUM

1 tub TANG Brand Orange Flavor Sugar Free Drink Mix
1½ cups cold low calorie cranberry juice cocktail
1 bottle (1 liter) cold diet ginger ale *or* club soda
Ice cubes

PLACE drink mix in large plastic or glass pitcher. Add juice; stir to dissolve. Refrigerate.

JUST before serving, pour into punch bowl. Stir in ginger ale and ice cubes.

Makes about 11 (½-cup) servings

Nutrition Information Per Serving: 10 calories, 0g total fat, 0g saturated fat, 0mg cholesterol, 20mg sodium, 2g carbohydrate, 0g dietary fiber, 2g sugars, 0g protein

70% daily value vitamin C

Exchange: FREE

KRAFT
Diabetic Choices

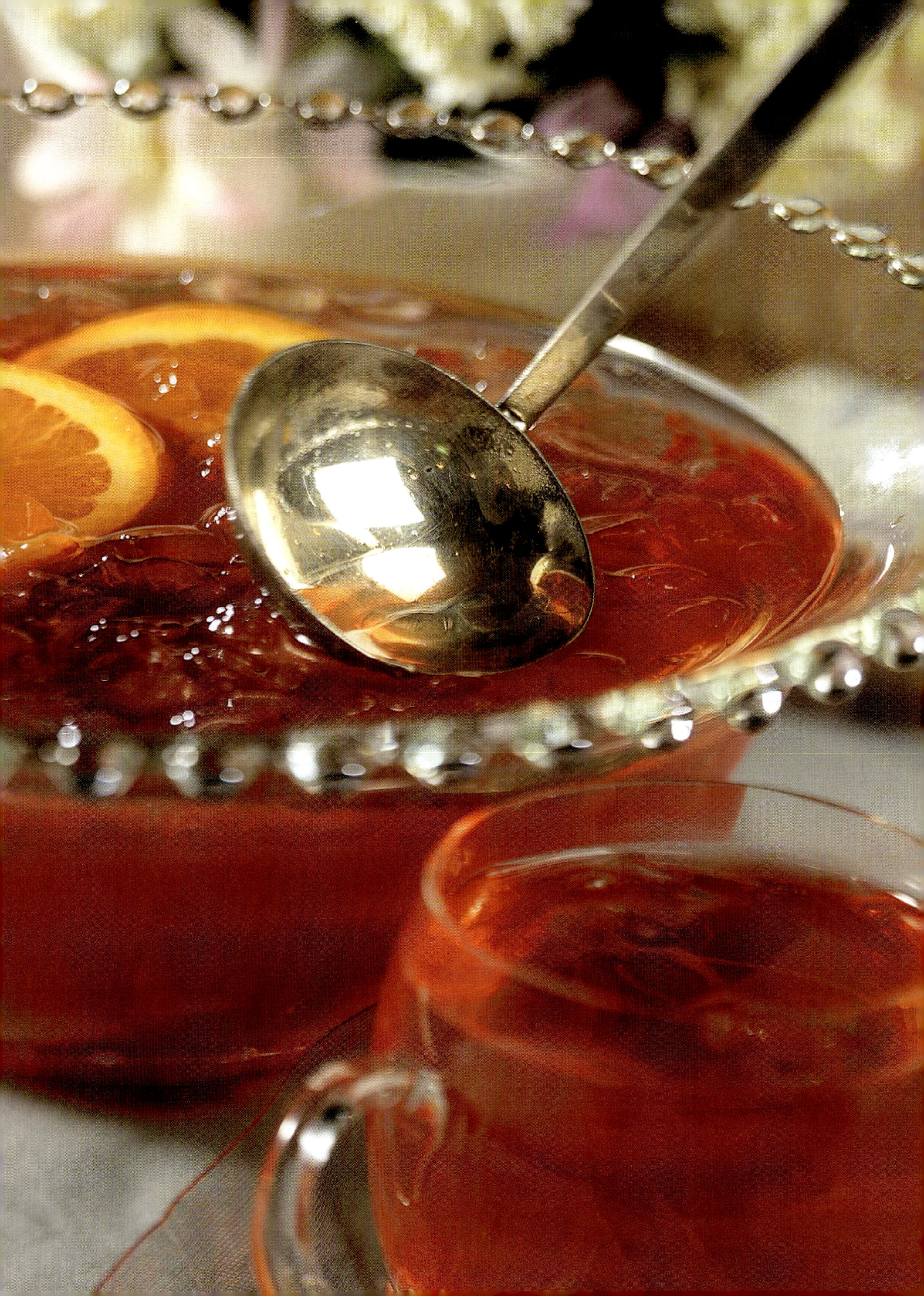

BEVERAGES

Cranberry Raspberry Breeze
Prep: 5 minutes

CALORIE   SODIUM

1 tub CRYSTAL LIGHT Raspberry Ice Flavor Low Calorie Soft Drink Mix
4 cups (1 quart) cold reduced calorie cranberry juice cocktail
1 bottle (1 liter) cold club soda
Ice cubes

PLACE drink mix in large plastic or glass pitcher. Add cranberry juice cocktail; stir to dissolve. Refrigerate.

JUST before serving, stir in club soda. Serve over ice.

Makes 8 (1-cup) servings

Nutrition Information Per Serving: 25 calories, 0g total fat, 0g saturated fat, 0mg cholesterol, 10mg sodium, 6g carbohydrate, 0g dietary fiber, 6g sugars, 0g protein

60% daily value vitamin C

Exchange: ½ Fruit

BEVERAGES

Coffee Shake

Prep: 5 minutes

2 cups cold fat free milk
1 cup fat free no sugar added vanilla, coffee or chocolate ice cream, softened
½ cup GENERAL FOODS INTERNATIONAL COFFEES Fat Free Sugar Free, French Vanilla Café Flavor

PLACE milk, ice cream and flavored instant coffee in blender; cover. Blend on high speed until smooth.

Makes 3 (1-cup) servings

Nutrition Information Per Serving: 170 calories, 1.5g total fat, 0.5g saturated fat, less than 5mg cholesterol, 240mg sodium, 31g carbohydrate, less than 1g dietary fiber, 12g sugars, 8g protein

25% daily value calcium

Exchange: 1 Carbohydrate, 1 Skim Milk

BEVERAGES

Strawberry-Banana Frappé
Prep: 5 minutes

1 pint (2 cups) vanilla frozen yogurt, softened
2 teaspoons CRYSTAL LIGHT with Calcium Strawberry Tangerine Flavor Low Calorie Soft Drink Mix *or any flavor*
1 cup strawberry halves
1 ripe banana, cut into chunks

PLACE all ingredients in blender container in order listed; cover. Blend on high speed until smooth.

Makes 6 (1-cup) servings

Note: Place remaining CRYSTAL LIGHT Drink Mix in glass or plastic pitcher. Add 5 cups cold water; stir to dissolve. Serve over ice.

Nutrition Information Per Serving: 110 calories, 3g total fat, 1.5g saturated fat, 0mg cholesterol, 45mg sodium, 18g carbohydrate, 1g dietary fiber, 15g sugars, 2g protein

15% daily value vitamin A, 45% daily value vitamin C, 20% daily value calcium

Exchange: 1 Carbohydrate, ½ Fat

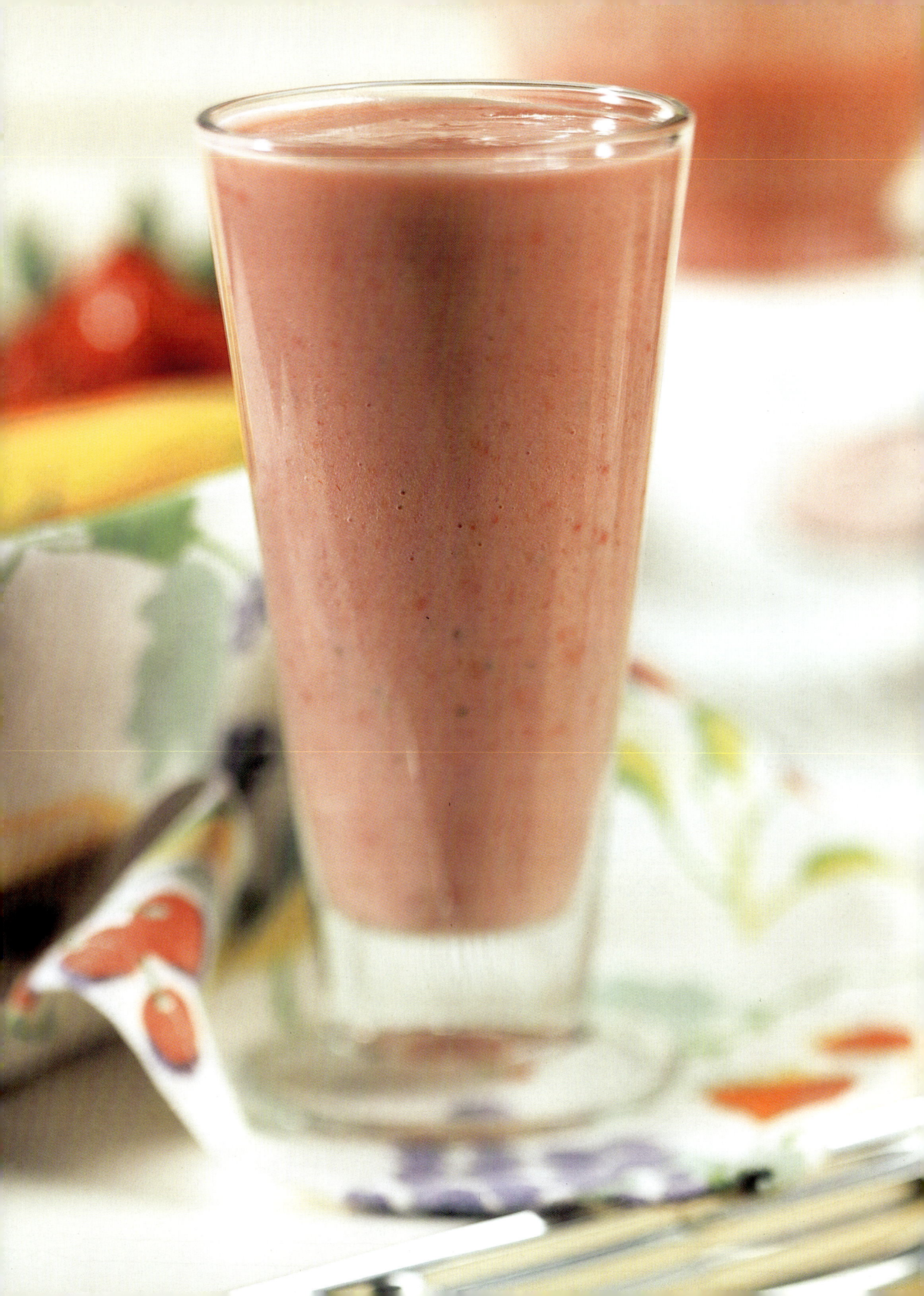

BEVERAGES

Citrus Cooler

Prep: 5 minutes

CALORIE   SODIUM

- 1 envelope KOOL-AID Sugar Free Lemonade Flavor Low Calorie Soft Drink Mix
- 2 cups cold water
- 2 cups cold orange juice
- 1 bottle (1 liter) cold diet lemon-lime carbonated beverage
- Ice cubes

PLACE drink mix in large plastic or glass pitcher. Add water and juice; stir to dissolve. Refrigerate until ready to serve.

JUST before serving, stir in carbonated beverage. Serve over ice.

Makes 8 (1-cup) servings

Nutrition Information Per Serving: 30 calories, 0g total fat, 0g saturated fat, 0mg cholesterol, 25mg sodium, 7g carbohydrate, 0g dietary fiber, 6g sugars, less than 1g protein

45% daily value vitamin C

Exchange: ½ Fruit

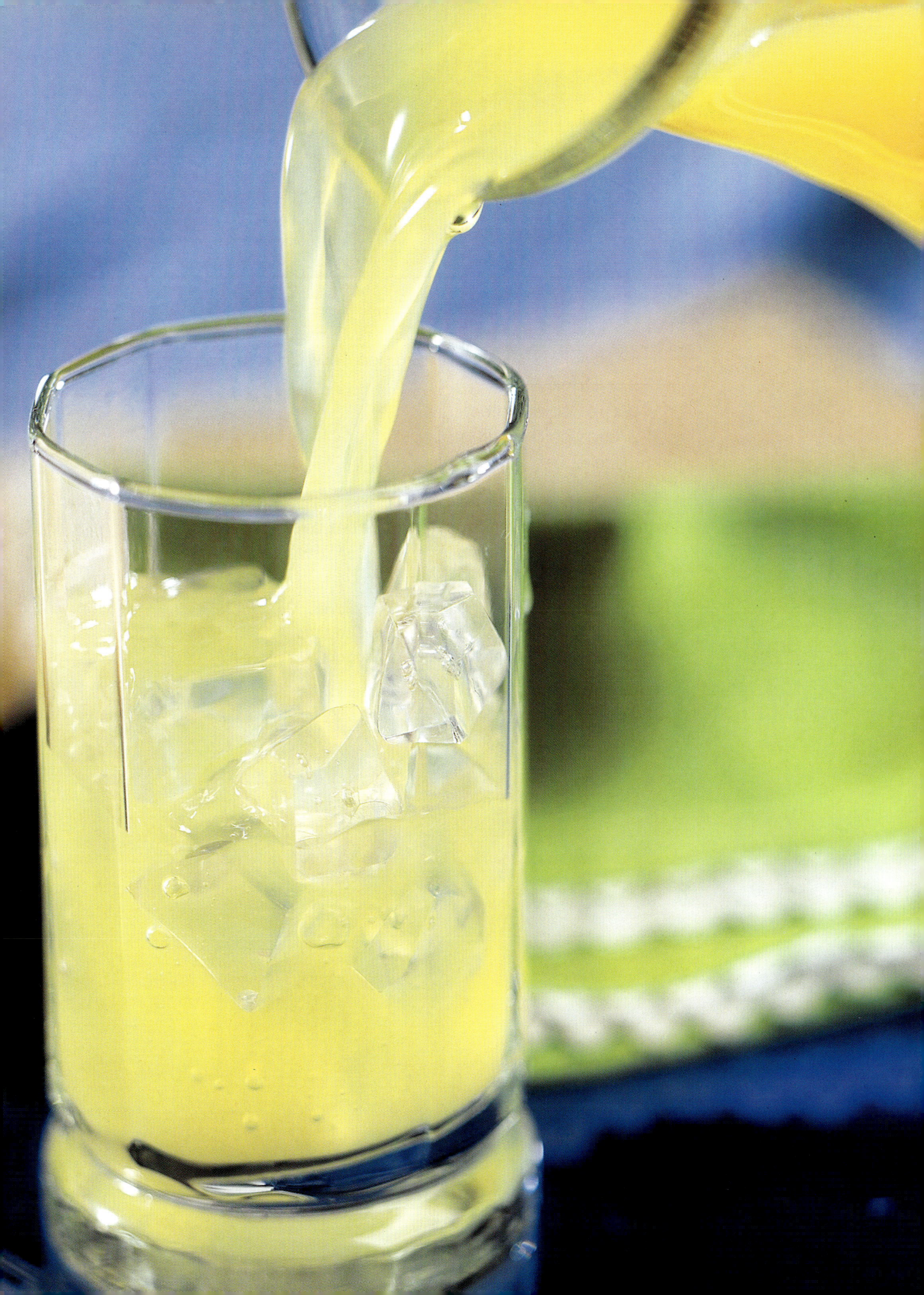

BEVERAGES

Iced Apple Tea

Prep: 5 minutes

▼ CALORIE   ▼ SODIUM

    1 tub CRYSTAL LIGHT Iced Tea Low Calorie Soft Drink Mix
    6 cups cold water
    2 cups cold apple juice
    Ice cubes

PLACE drink mix in large plastic or glass pitcher. Add water and juice; stir to dissolve. Serve over ice.

Makes 8 (1-cup) servings

Nutrition Information Per Serving: 30 calories, 0g total fat, 0g saturated fat, 0mg cholesterol, 10mg sodium, 8g carbohydrate, 0g dietary fiber, 7g sugars, 0g protein

Exchange: ½ Fruit

BEVERAGES

Berry Lemonade
Prep: 5 minutes

CALORIE   SODIUM

6 cups cold water, divided
1 package (12 ounces) frozen unsweetened raspberries
1 tub COUNTRY TIME Lemonade Flavor Sugar Free Low Calorie Drink Mix

PLACE 3 cups of the water, raspberries and drink mix in blender container; cover. Blend on high speed until smooth; strain fruit mixture to remove seeds. Pour into large plastic or glass pitcher. Stir in remaining 3 cups water.

REFRIGERATE until ready to serve. Stir before serving.

Makes 8 (1-cup) servings

Strawberry Lemonade: Substitute 1 package (12 ounces) frozen unsweetened strawberries for raspberries. Do not strain fruit mixture.

Nutrition Information Per Serving: 25 calories, 0g total fat, 0g saturated fat, 0mg cholesterol, 5mg sodium, 5g carbohydrate, less than 1g dietary fiber, 4g sugars, 0g protein

25% daily value vitamin C

Exchange: ½ Fruit

BEVERAGES

Hot Cappuccino Float
Prep: 5 minutes

¼ cup fat free no sugar added vanilla flavored ice cream
1 envelope GENERAL FOODS INTERNATIONAL COFFEES Sugar Free Cappuccino, any flavor
1 cup hot fat free milk

PLACE ice cream in large cup or mug. Prepare Cappuccino as directed on package, substituting hot milk for the water. Pour over ice cream. Serve immediately.

Makes 1 serving

Nutrition Information Per Serving: 190 calories, 3.5g total fat, 1g saturated fat, less than 5mg cholesterol, 230mg sodium, 28g carbohydrate, 0g dietary fiber, 15g sugars, 11g protein

10% daily value vitamin A, 35% daily value calcium

Exchange: 1 Carbohydrate, 1 Low Fat Milk

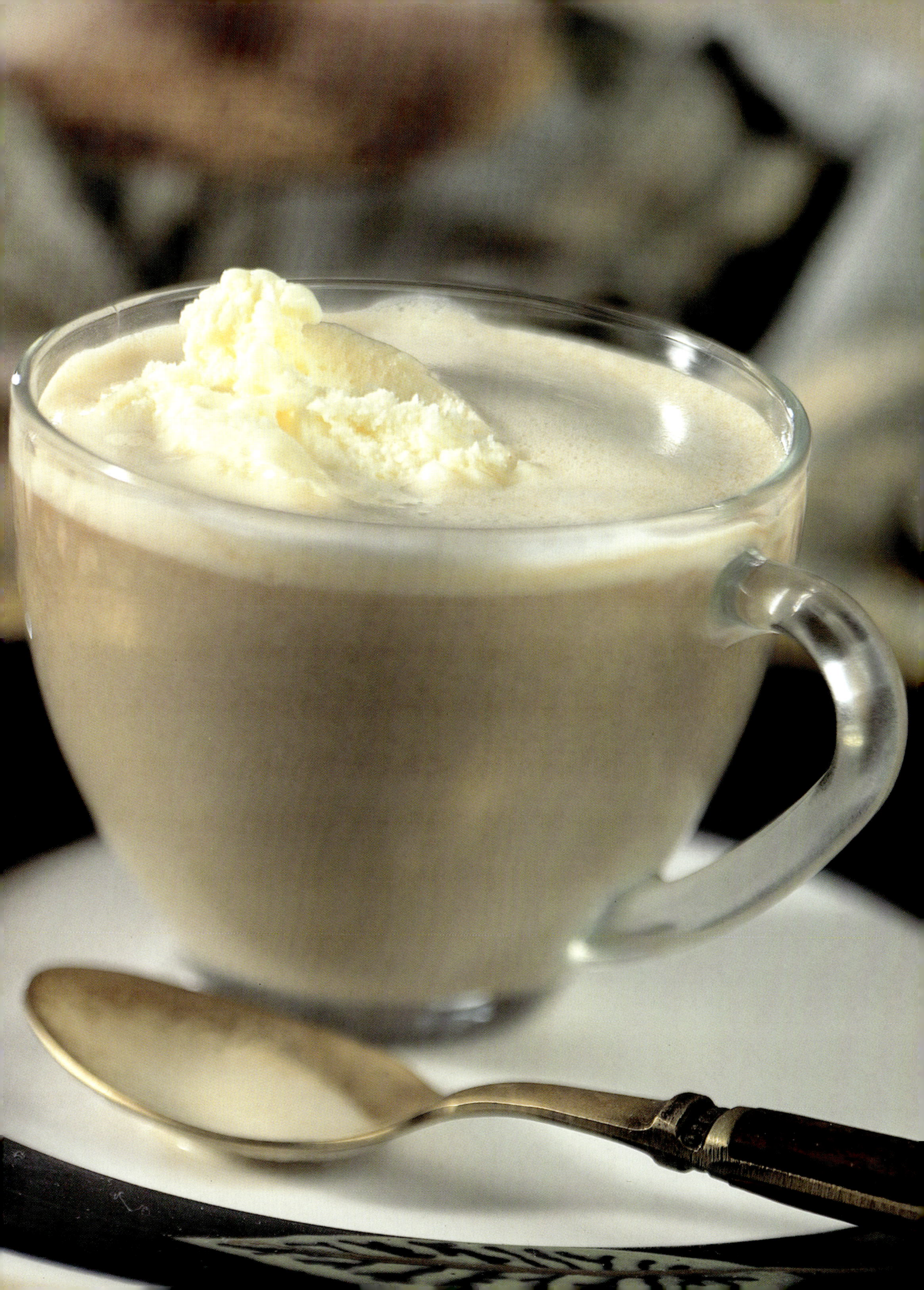

SNACKS & DIPS

Black Forest Snack
Prep: 5 minutes

8 fat free brownies (2¾ × 2¾ inches)
1 can (21 ounces) light cherry pie filling
2 cups thawed COOL WHIP LITE Whipped Topping

SPOON ¼ cup of the pie filling over each brownie.

TOP each with ¼ cup whipped topping.

SERVE immediately or refrigerate until ready to serve.

Makes 8 servings

Nutrition Information Per Serving: 220 calories, 3g total fat, 3g saturated fat, 0mg cholesterol, 85mg sodium, 46g carbohydrate, 1g dietary fiber, 35g sugars, 3g protein

Exchange: 3 Carbohydrate

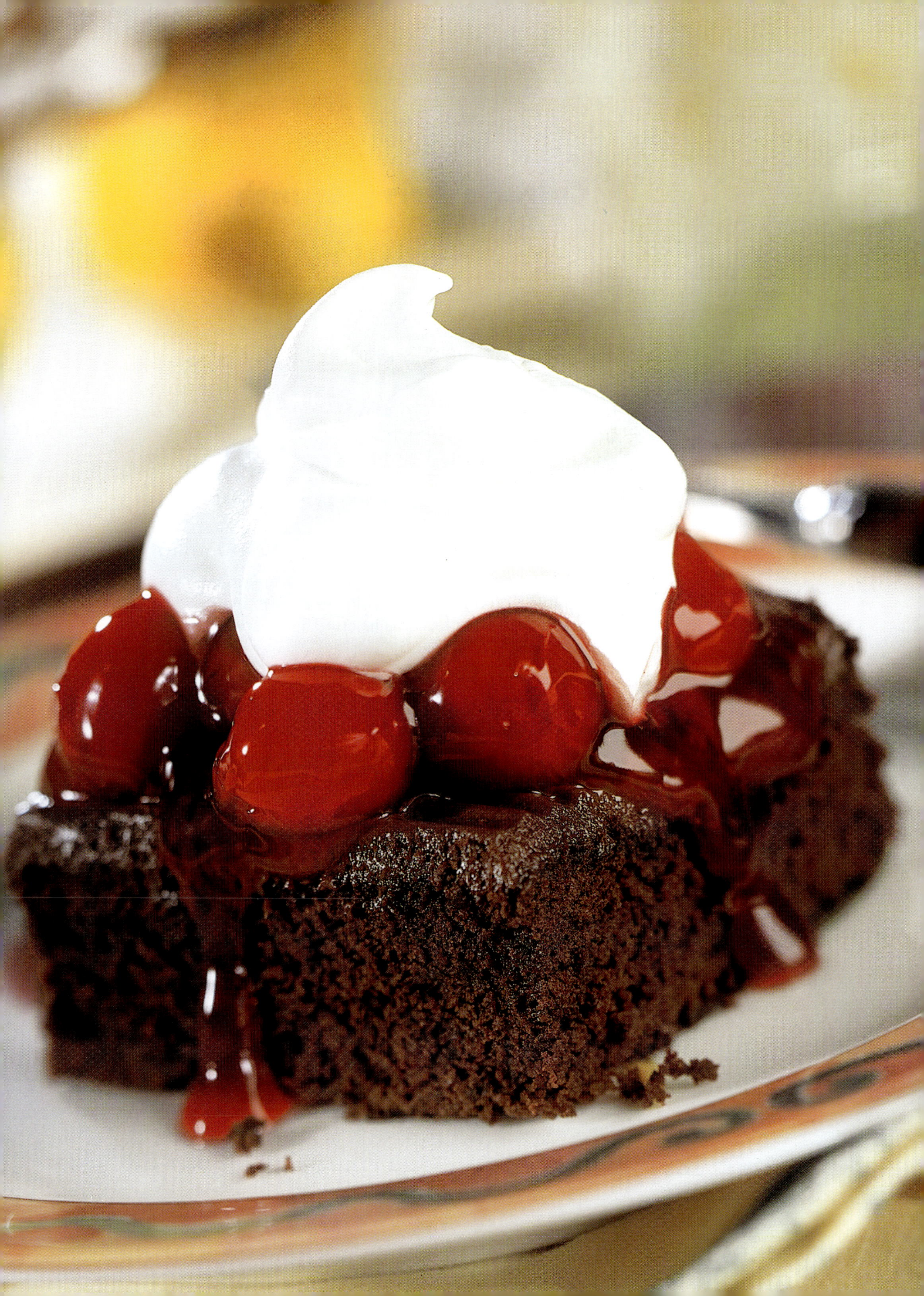

SNACKS & DIPS

Cottage Berry Crunch

Prep: 5 minutes

½ cup BREAKSTONE'S *or* KNUDSEN 2% Cottage Cheese
2 tablespoons low fat granola
½ banana, sliced
½ cup assorted berries

SPOON cottage cheese onto serving plate. Sprinkle with granola. Top with fruit.

Makes 1 serving

Special Extra: The beauty of this dish is that you can cut up virtually any fruit you have on hand to serve with the cottage cheese. For extra flavor and crunch, try sprinkling with your favorite POST Cereal.

Nutrition Information Per Serving: 220 calories, 3.5g total fat, 2g saturated fat, 15mg cholesterol, 430mg sodium, 34g carbohydrate, 5g dietary fiber, 20g sugars, 15g protein

50% daily value vitamin C

Exchange: 2 Fruit, 2 Lean Meat

SNACKS & DIPS

Tropical Snack Mix

Prep: 5 minutes

4 cups POST SPOON SIZE Shredded Wheat *or* POST SPOON SIZE Frosted Shredded Wheat *or* POST SPOON SIZE Honey Nut Shredded Wheat Cereal

2 cups dried fruit mix (such as prune, apricot, pear), chopped

1 cup BAKER'S ANGEL FLAKE Coconut

MIX all ingredients in large bowl.

Makes about 16 (½-cup) servings

Fun With The Kids: Let the kids mix this up, allowing them to choose which of the dried fruit to use in the mix. Then let them spoon the mix into zipper-style plastic bags to take along as snacks.

Nutrition Information Per Serving: 120 calories, 3g total fat, 2.5g saturated fat, 0mg cholesterol, 25mg sodium, 25g carbohydrate, 4g dietary fiber, 13g sugars, 2g protein

10% daily value vitamin A

Exchange: ½ Starch, 1 Fruit, ½ Fat

SNACKS & DIPS

Grab 'n Go Peanut Butter Bars

Prep: 10 minutes   Microwave: 1½ minutes

½ cup firmly packed brown sugar
½ cup honey
½ cup reduced fat peanut butter
3 cups POST SPOON SIZE Shredded Wheat Cereal, coarsely crushed
¾ cup raisins

SPRAY 8-inch square baking pan with no stick cooking spray.

MIX sugar, honey and peanut butter in 2-quart microwavable bowl. Microwave on HIGH 1½ to 2 minutes or until bubbly at edges; stir until smooth.

STIR in crushed cereal and raisins. Press firmly into prepared baking pan.

COOL. Cut into bars. Store in airtight container.

Makes 16 bars

Use Your Stove: Heat sugar, honey and peanut butter in large saucepan on medium heat until smooth and bubbly, stirring occasionally. Stir in cereal and raisins. Press into greased 8-inch square baking pan. Cool. Cut into bars. Store in airtight container.

Take Along Tip: After completely cooled, wrap individual bars in plastic wrap. Left in a bowl on the kitchen counter, they make a great grab-and-go snack.

Nutrition Information Per Bar: 160 calories, 3.5g total fat, 0.5g saturated fat, 0mg cholesterol, 50mg sodium, 31g carbohydrate, 2g dietary fiber, 20g sugars, 4g protein

Exchange: 1½ Starch, ½ Fat

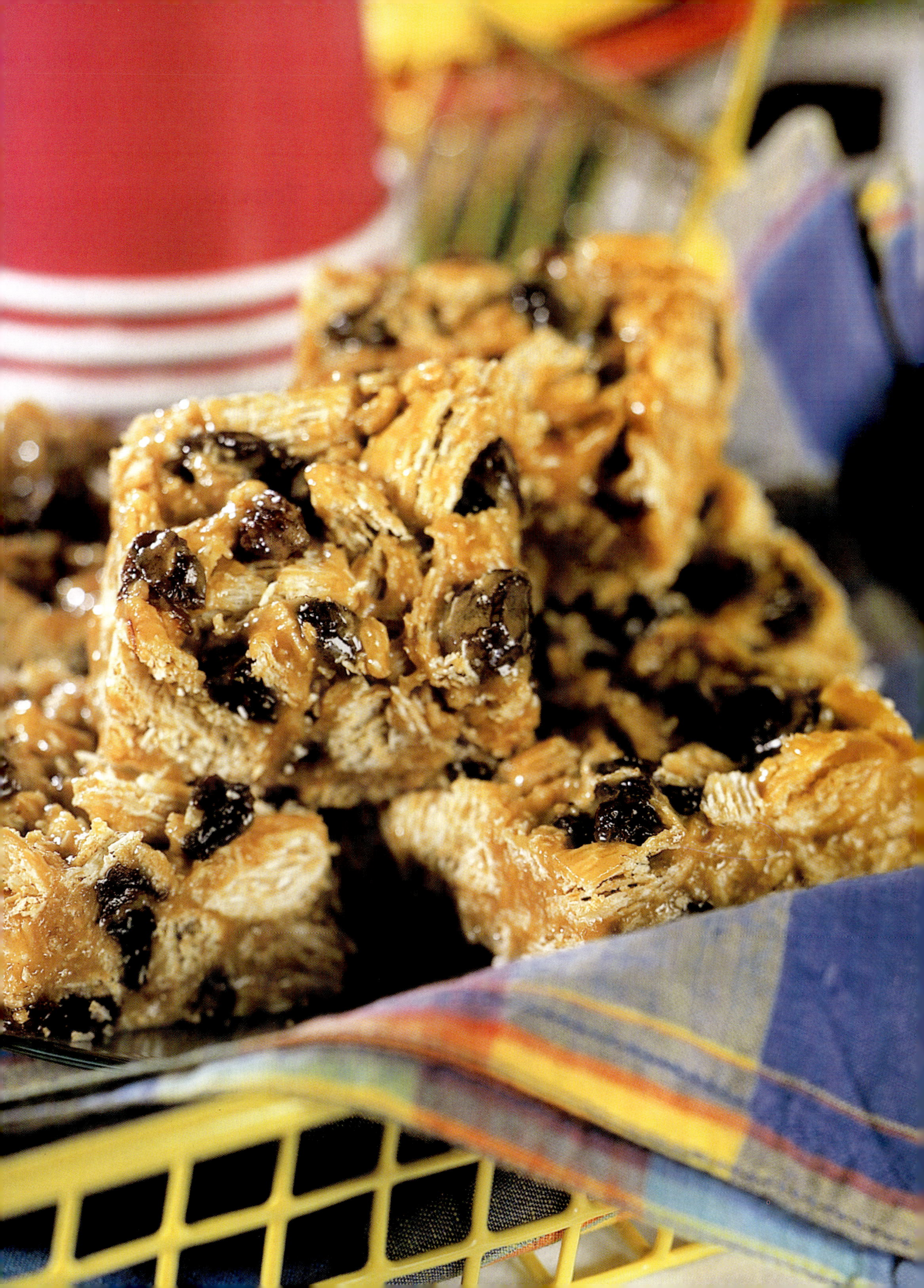

SNACKS & DIPS

Frozen Shortbread Treats
Prep: 10 minutes plus freezing

SODIUM

1 cup COOL WHIP LITE Whipped Topping
16 SNACKWELL'S Sugar Free Shortbread Cookies

SPREAD 2 tablespoons whipped topping on each of 8 cookies. Press remaining cookies lightly on top, making sandwiches.

FREEZE about 3 hours or until firm. Wrap individually. Store in freezer for up to 3 days.

Makes 8 treats

Nutrition Information Per Treat: 110 calories, 5g total fat, 2g saturated fat, less than 5mg cholesterol, 105mg sodium, 17g carbohydrate, 0g dietary fiber, 2g sugars, 1g protein

Exchange: 1 Carbohydrate, 1 Fat

SNACKS & DIPS

SPOON SIZE® Reduced Fat Munch Mix

Prep: 5 minutes   Bake: 30 minutes

4 cups POST SPOON SIZE Shredded Wheat Cereal
1 cup small unsalted pretzels
1 cup popped popcorn
3 tablespoons 70% vegetable oil spread, melted
1 tablespoon Worcestershire sauce
1 teaspoon seasoned salt

HEAT oven to 350°F.

MIX cereal, pretzels and popcorn in 15×10×1-inch baking pan.

MIX spread, Worcestershire sauce and seasoned salt in small bowl. Drizzle evenly over cereal mixture; toss to coat.

BAKE 30 minutes or until crisp, stirring halfway through baking time. Cool. Store in tightly covered containers.

Makes 12 (½-cup) servings

Use Your Microwave: Prepare mixture as directed. Pour into large microwavable bowl. Microwave on HIGH 5 to 6 minutes or until crisp, stirring halfway through cooking time.

Nutrition Information Per Serving: 100 calories, 3g total fat, 0.5g saturated fat, 0mg cholesterol, 190mg sodium, 17g carbohydrate, 2g dietary fiber, 0g sugars, 2g protein

Exchange: 1 Starch, ½ Fat

SNACKS & DIPS

Tropical Fruit Dip

Prep: 5 minutes

1 tub CRYSTAL LIGHT TROPICAL PASSIONS Low Calorie Soft Drink Mix, any flavor
4 containers (8 ounces each) BREYERS® Vanilla Lowfat Yogurt

STIR drink mix into yogurt in medium bowl until well blended. Serve as a dip with assorted fresh fruit.

Makes 4 cups

Nutrition Information Per Serving (2 tablespoons): 30 calories, 0g total fat, 0g saturated fat, less than 5mg cholesterol, 15mg sodium, 5g carbohydrate, 0g dietary fiber, 5g sugars, 1g protein

Exchange: ½ Carbohydrate

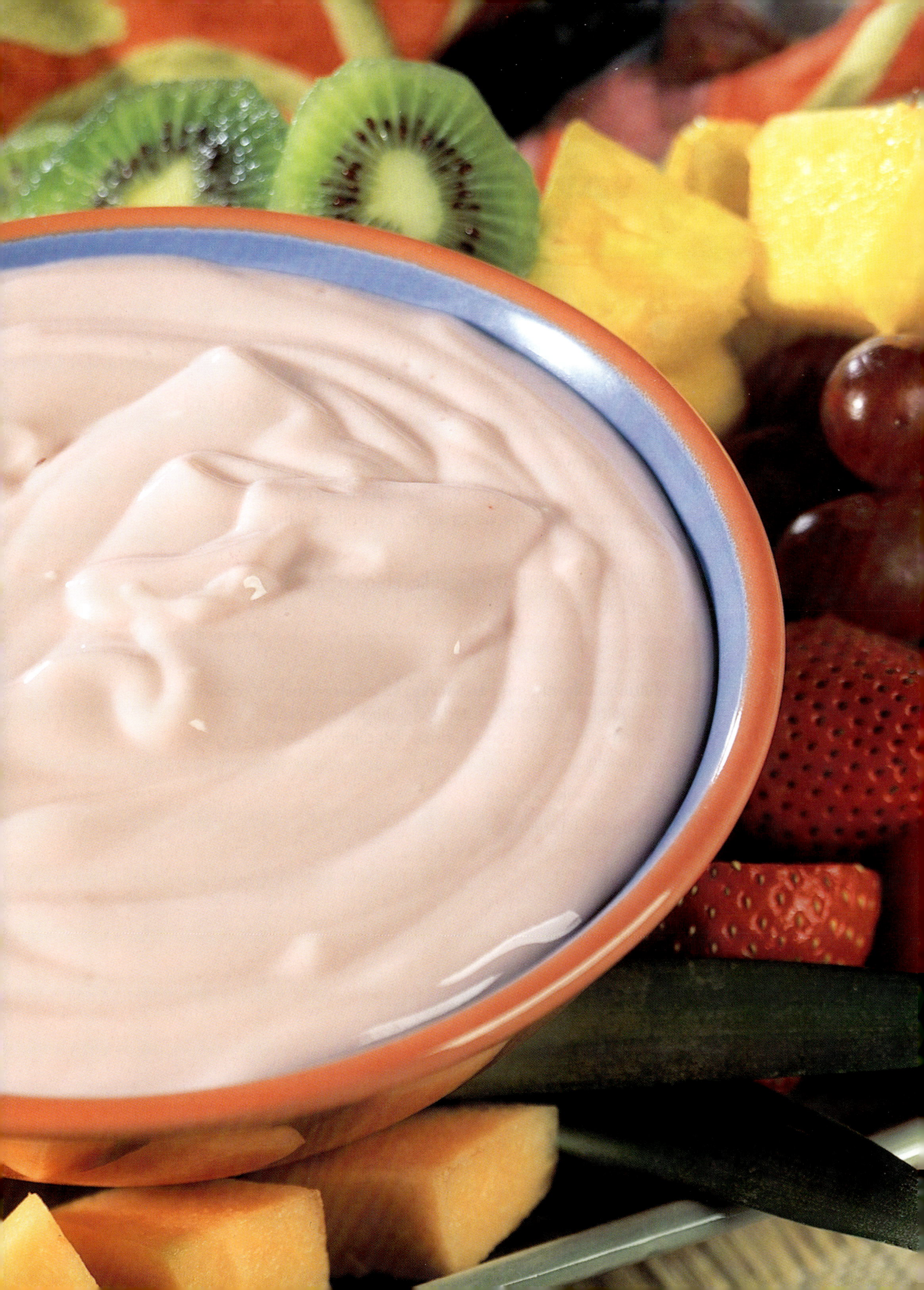

SNACKS & DIPS

VELVETA LIGHT® Salsa Dip
Prep: 5 minutes   Microwave: 5 minutes

1 pound (16 ounces) VELVEETA LIGHT Pasteurized Prepared Cheese Product, cut up
1 cup TACO BELL® HOME ORIGINALS® Thick 'N Chunky Salsa

MICROWAVE process cheese product and salsa in 1½-quart microwavable bowl on HIGH 5 minutes or until prepared cheese product is melted, stirring after 3 minutes.

SERVE hot with baked tortilla chips or assorted cut-up vegetables.

Makes 3 cups

Nutrition Information Per Serving (2 tablespoons): 50 calories, 2.5g total fat, 1.5g saturated fat, 10mg cholesterol, 440mg sodium, 4g carbohydrate, 0g dietary fiber, 2g sugars, 5g protein

15% daily value calcium

Exchange: 1 Lean Meat

Snacks & Dips

Cheesy Spinach Dip
Prep: 5 minutes   Microwave: 7 minutes

1 pound (16 ounces) VELVEETA LIGHT Pasteurized Prepared Cheese Product, cut up
1 can (14½ ounces) tomatoes, whole, cut up, drained
1 package (10 ounces) frozen chopped spinach, thawed, drained
¼ teaspoon red pepper flakes

MICROWAVE prepared cheese product and tomatoes in 1-quart microwavable bowl on HIGH 5 minutes or until prepared cheese product is completely melted, stirring after 2 minutes.

STIR in remaining ingredients. Microwave on HIGH 2 minutes or until thoroughly heated. Serve hot with bread sticks, tortilla chips or assorted cut-up vegetables.

Makes 3 cups

Nutrition Information Per Serving (2 tablespoons): 45 calories, 2g total fat, 1.5g saturated fat, 10mg cholesterol, 330mg sodium, 3g carbohydrate, 0g dietary fiber, 2g sugars, 4g protein

20% daily value vitamin A, 10% daily value calcium

Exchange: ½ Skim Milk

INDEX

Apple Cranberry Mold, 34
Apples
  Double Apple Bran Cereal Muffins, 14
  Shredded Wheat Autumn Crisp, 46
Applesauce
  Applesauce Muffins, 13
  Double Apple Bran Cereal Muffins, 14
Applesauce Muffins, 13

Bacon: Grilled Chicken Spinach Salad, 38
Bananas
  Chocolate Banana Split, 61
  Cottage Berry Crunch, 82
  Strawberry-Banana Frappé, 72
  Yogurt Crunch Parfaits, 54
Beans
  BOCA® Chili, 26
  Fresh Garden Spinach Salad, 42
  Tuscan Vegetable Potato Salad, 43
Bell Peppers
  BOCA® Chili, 26
  Chicken Brown Rice Primavera, 24
  Fresh Garden Spinach Salad, 42
Berries
  Berry Lemonade, 77
  Cottage Berry Crunch, 82
  Peach Melba Dessert, 52
  Strawberry-Banana Frappé, 72
  Waffle Stack, 12
Berry Lemonade, 77
Black Forest Snack, 80
BOCA® Chili, 26
BOCA® Pasta Bake, 29
Boo Cups, 50
Breads
  Applesauce Muffins, 13
  Double Apple Bran Cereal Muffins, 14
  Lemony Wheatful Fruit Bread, 10
  Low Fat Orange-Raisin Bran Bread, 16
Breakfast Burrito, 17
Breakfast Quesadilla, 8
Broccoli
  Chicken Brown Rice Primavera, 24
  Fresh Garden Spinach Salad, 42

Café Pudding, 55
Cakes: Chocolate Pudding Poke Cake, 66
California Baked Potatoes, 32
Cereal Yogurt Bars, 60

Cheese
  BOCA® Pasta Bake, 29
  Breakfast Burrito, 17
  Cheesy Rice, 36
  Cheesy Spinach Dip, 92
  Cottage Cheese Zucchini Casserole, 40
  Down Home Macaroni & Cheese, 22
  Spinach Lasagna, 20
  VELVEETA LIGHT® Easy Pasta Primavera, 21
  VELVEETA LIGHT® Salsa Dip, 90
Cheesy Deluxe Primavera Mac Skillet, 30
Cheesy Spinach Dip, 92
Cheesy Rice, 36
Chicken
  Chicken Brown Rice Primavera, 24
  Grilled Chicken Spinach Salad, 38
  20 Minute Garlic Rasemary Chicken & Brown Rice Dinner, 28
Chocolate
  Black Forest Snack, 80
  Chocolate Banana Split, 61
  Chocolate Pudding Poke Cake, 66
  Double Chocolate Bread Pudding, 56
Chocolate Banana Split, 61
Chocolate Pudding Poke Cake, 66
Citrus Cooler, 74
Coffee Shake, 71
Cookies
  Cereal Yogurt Bars, 60
  Frozen Shortbread Treats, 86
  Grab 'n Go Peanut Butter Bars, 84
Cottage Berry Crunch, 82
Cottage Cheese
  Cottage Berry Crunch, 82
  Cottage Cheese Zucchini Casserole, 40
  Crunchy Tuna Salad, 37
  Low Fat Lemon Soufflé Cheesecake, 48
  Spinach Lasagna, 20
  Waffle Stack, 12
Cottage Cheese Zucchini Casserole, 40
Cranberry Raspberry Breeze, 70
Cream Cheese
  Easy Tiramisu, 62
  Low Fat Lemon Soufflé Cheesecake, 48
  Peach Melba Dessert, 52
Creamy Mexican Mold, 44
Crunchy Tuna Salad, 37

93

Index

Double Apple Bran Cereal Muffins, 14
Double Chocolate Bread Pudding, 56
Down Home Macaroni & Cheese, 22

Easy Tiramisu, 62

Fresh Garden Spinach Salad, 42
Frozen Shortbread Treats, 86
Fruit (see also **Apples; Bananas; Berries; Oranges**)
  Black Forest Snack, 80
  Paradise Parfaits, 58
  Peach Melba Dessert, 52
  Yogurt Crunch Parfaits, 54

Grab 'n Go Peanut Butter Bars, 84
Grilled Chicken Spinach Salad, 38

Hot Cappuccino Float, 78

Iced Apple Tea, 76

Lemon
  Berry Lemonade, 77
  Citrus Cooler, 74
  Lemony Wheatful Fruit Bread, 10
  Low Fat Lemon Soufflé Cheesecake, 48
Low Fat Lemon Soufflé Cheesecake, 48
Low Fat Orange-Raisin Bran Bread, 16

Mushrooms
  Cottage Cheese Zucchini Casserole, 40
  Grilled Chicken Spinach Salad, 38

Nugget Parmigiana Sub, 18

Orange
  Citrus Cooler, 74
  Low Fat Orange-Raisin Bran Bread, 16
  Sunset Punch, 68

Paradise Parfaits, 58
Pasta
  BOCA® Pasta Bake, 29
  Cheesy Deluxe Primavera Mac Skillet, 30
  Down Home Macaroni & Cheese, 22
  Spinach Lasagna, 20
  VELVEETA LIGHT® Easy Pasta Primavera, 21

Peach Melba Dessert, 52
Peanut Butter and Jam Parfaits, 64
Potatoes
  California Baked Potatoes, 32
  Tuscan Vegetable Potato Salad, 43

Rice
  Cheesy Rice, 36
  Chicken Brown Rice Primavera, 24
  20 Minute Garlic Rasemary Chicken & Brown Rice Dinner, 28

Sandwiches: Nugget Parmigiana Sub, 18
Shredded Wheat Autumn Crisp, 46
Spinach
  Cheesy Spinach Dip, 92
  Fresh Garden Spinach Salad, 42
  Grilled Chicken Spinach Salad, 38
  Spinach Lasagna, 20
SPOON SIZE® Reduced Fat Munch Mix, 87
Strawberry-Banana Frappé, 72
Sunset Punch, 68

Tomatoes, Fresh
  Crunchy Tuna Salad, 37
  Fresh Garden Spinach Salad, 42
Tropical Fruit Dip, 88
Tropical Snack Mix, 83
Tuna: Crunchy Tuna Salad, 37
Tuscan Vegetable Potato Salad, 43
20 Minute Garlic Rasemary Chicken & Brown Rice Dinner, 28

VELVEETA LIGHT® Easy Pasta Primavera, 21
VELVEETA LIGHT® Salsa Dip, 90

Waffle Stack, 12

Yogurt Crunch Parfaits, 54

Zucchini: Cottage Cheese Zucchini Casserole, 40